SPANISH

Complete Revision Guide

Niobe O'Connor

Published by BBC Active, an imprint of Educational Publishers LLP, part of the Pearson Education Group
Edinburgh Gate, Harlow, Essex CN20 2JE, England

© Niobe O'Connor/BBC Worldwide Ltd, 2002

BBC logo © BBC 1996. BBC and BBC Active are trademarks of the British Broadcasting Corporation

ISBN: 978-1-4066-1368-1

Printed in China GCC/01

The Publisher's policy is to use paper manufactured from sustainable forests.

First published 2002
This edition 2007

Contents

Young person in society

Introduction

About Bitesize

GCSE Bitesize is a revision service designed to help you achieve success at GCSE. There are books, television programmes and a website, each of which provides a separate resource designed to help you get the best results.

The website can be found at http://www.bbc.co.uk/schools/gcsebitesize

About this book

This book is your all-in-one revision companion for GCSE. It gives you the three things you need for successful revision:

1 Every topic clearly organised and clearly explained.

2 The most important facts and ideas pulled out for **quick checking**: in each topic and in the extra sections at the end of this book.

3 All the practice you need: in the 'check' questions in the margins, in the question sections at the end of each topic, and in the exam practice section at the end of this book.

Each topic is organised in the same way:

■ The Bare Bones: a reminder of the main themes to revise

■ Key ideas highlighted throughout

■ Check questions in the margin: mini-tasks to try

■ Remember tips and Exam tips

■ Practice questions at the end of each topic

The extra sections at the back of this book will help you check your progress and be confident that you know your stuff:

Exam questions and model answers

■ A range of exam questions with suggested answers.

■ Extra questions for you to complete (answers at the end).

Topic checker

■ Reminders of what you need to be able to do in each topic.

■ As you revise each topic, try answering each question. Put ticks or crosses next to it.

About this book (continued)

- The next time you revise that topic, try the questions again.

- Do this until you've got a column of ticks.

Complete the grammar
- Another resource for you to use as you revise: fill in the gaps to complete the grammar facts.

Last-minute learner
- A mini-book that you can cut out, containing all the most important ideas in just four pages.

About your exam

Get organised
You need to know when your exams are, before you can make your revision plan.

- Check the dates and times of your exams with your teacher, tutor or school-office. Remember you probably have a Speaking, Listening, Reading and Writing exam.

- The Speaking part will almost certainly be the first, and come rather earlier than the others - possibly before Easter.

- Make sure you have the dates written down in large writing somewhere very visible in your bedroom - it's easy to think you have more time to revise than you actually have!

Check the exam details
- Check with your teacher exactly what you have to do for each part of the exam, especially the Speaking part. Do you have to do a presentation? How many role-plays? How long is the conversation part?

- Find out if you're allowed a dictionary during the preparation time, how long it is, and whether you're allowed to take any notes you make during that time into the exam with you.

- Make sure you know exactly which sections of the exam you're entering: there are usually Foundation and Higher papers, and you may be able to choose a combination which plays to your particular strengths. Some boards allow you to make a decision on the day of the Speaking test itself as to whether you do the Higher part or not - does yours?

Planning your revision

Be clear about what you have to revise.

- Find out if your exam board produces a student guide. It will tell you exactly what you need to know: topics, vocabulary, grammar. Your teacher may be able to help you order one, or have copies put in the library.

- Make a list of all the topics you need to cover. Highlight the ones which you may need to revise first for your speaking exam: topics you may be asked about in the conversation or presentation part of the exam (e.g. personal information, family, school), or in the role-plays (e.g. being a guest or welcoming a visitor, eating out, buying tickets).

- Organise your work into topic areas, so that you have everything you need in one place. Each topic area might have vocabulary lists, activities from class and homework, and any grammar which is particularly useful.

- Count the number of days left, and decide how you're going to allocate your revision time.

- In Bitesize Spanish, there are four main sections of 18 pages each, and an additional listening section of 12 pages. How many pages will you tackle a week? Break it down into days, then hours and minutes.

- Don't make your revision sessions too long - it is often better to do a small amount every day, rather than a larger chunk once a week. Draw up an action plan for yourself and try to stick to it.

Get started

Once you've made your plan, start work. When you revise, make sure that:

- you've got a quiet place to work

- you've got all you need: video, book, pencil, a dictionary, internet access ...

- you don't allow yourself to be distracted by the TV, the radio, magazines ...

- you keep the revision session short and focused, so you avoid getting tired or demotivated.

Using this book

- There are four main themes, each covering six topic areas, in this book:
- 4 pages of vocabulary and grammar
- 6 pages covering the first three topics, of speaking, reading and writing activities
- 2 pages of vocabulary and grammar
- 6 pages, covering the next three topics of speaking, reading and writing activities

Using this book (continued)

- There is also a separate listening section after the four main themes. It contains a variety of exam-type activities, based on the Bitesize Revision TV programmes which you can video. Check the Bitesize website for when they will be shown.

Each topic in Bitesize Spanish has two pages. Here are some ideas to help you revise it.

- When you decide which topic you are going to revise, you might like to have your school-work or text-book on the same topic nearby so you can jot down any extra things.

- Read through the helpful words and phrases for your topic on the relevant vocabulary page. Cover up the English side and see how many you can remember, then do the same with the Spanish side.

- Read the grammar, and do the activities. Don't forget to check your answers at the back!

- Work your way through the activities on the two pages. The 'quick' questions in the margin will help to keep you focused.

- When you've completed them, use the Topic checker at the back for that topic to make sure you've covered all main things you need to know.

- At the start of your next revision section, begin with the Topic checker for your previous topic: how many things can you do now?

On the day

Here are a few helpful hints for the day(s) of the exam:

- Make sure you know when your exam is (morning or afternoon), and where.

- Aim to arrive in plenty of time, with everything you need: several pens, a pencil, a ruler and - if allowed - your dictionary. There is usually someone who forgets theirs: make sure it isn't you!

- On your way or while you're waiting, read through your Last-minute Learner.

If you have time, listen to some Spanish on cassette to get yourself into a Spanish 'mood'.

Good luck with your revision - and good luck in your exam.

¡Buena suerte a todos!

Vocabulary

A Personal information

Remember
For the second or third of the month, simply use el dos, el tres.

¿Cómo te llamas? Me llamo ...	What's your name? I'm called ...
Mi nombre/apellido es ...	My first name/surname is ...
¿Cuántos años tienes? Tengo ... años.	How old are you? I'm ... years old.
¿Cuándo es tu cumpleaños?	When is your birthday?
Es el (primero/uno) (dos/tres) de mayo.	It's the (first) (second/third) of May.
¿De qué nacionalidad eres?	What nationality are you?
Soy (galés/galesa, inglés/inglesa).	I'm (Welsh, English).

a	(ah)	g	(hay)	m	(emay)	r	(erray)	x	(aykees)
b	(bay)	h	(atch-ay)	n	(enay)	s	(essay)	y	(ee gree ay ga)
c	(thay)	i	(ee)	ñ	(enyay)	t	(tay)	z	(thay ta)
d	(day)	j	(hotta)	o	(oh)	u	(oo)		
e	(ay)	k	(ka)	p	(pay)	v	(oovay)	¿Cómo se escribe?
f	(effay)	l	(elay)	q	(coo)	w	(oovay doblay)	Se escribe ...

(m)	(f)		(m)	(f)	
escocés	escocesa	*Scottish*	andaluz	andaluza	*Andalucian*
galés	galesa	*Welsh*	español	española	*Spanish*
inglés	inglesa	*English*	castellano	castellana	*Castillian*
irlandés	irlandesa	*Irish*	europeo	europea	*European*
francés	francesa	*French*	gallego	gallega	*Galician*
alemán	alemana	*German*	italiano	italiana	*Italian*
catalán	catalana	*Catalan*	americano	americana	*American*

B Family and friends

¿Cuántas personas hay en tu familia?	How many people are in your family?
Somos (cinco).	There are (five) of us.
¿Quiénes son? Hay ...	Who are they? There's ...
Mis padres están separados/divorciados.	My parents are separated/divorced.
soltero/a, casado/a, viudo/a.	single, married, a widower/widow
¿Tienes hermanos?	Have you got brothers and sisters?
Sí, tengo ... Soy hijo único/hija única.	Yes, I have ... I'm an only son/daughter.

Remember
With soltero/a, casado/a, viudo/a use the verb ser.
E.g. Es soltero.
(He is single.)

madre	*mother*	padres	*parents*	primo/a	*cousin*
madrastra	*step-mother*	abuelo	*grandfather*	hombre	*man*
padre	*father*	abuela	*grandmother*	mujer	*woman*
padrastro	*step-father*	tío/tía	*uncle/aunt*	chico	*boy*
hermano	*brother*	esposo/a	*husband/wife*	chica	*girl*
hermanastro	*step-brother*	marido	*husband*	amigo/a	*friend*
hermana	*sister*	joven	*young person*	novio	*boyfriend*
hermanastra	*step-sister*	sobrino/a	*nephew/niece*	novia	*girlfriend*

C   Interests and hobbies

¿Qué deportes practicas?	What sports do you play?
Juego al fútbol/al baloncesto.	I play football/basketball.
Practico el atletismo/el piragüismo.	I do athletics/canoeing.
Hago gimnasia/judo/aerobic.	I do gymnastics, judo, aerobics.
Hago ciclismo/vela/footing.	I go cycling/sailing/jogging.
¿Qué haces en tu tiempo libre?	What do you do in your free time?
Escucho música, leo libros/revistas.	I listen to music, read books/magazines.
Veo la tele, salgo con mis amigos.	I watch TV, I go out with my friends.
Navego por Internet, voy de paseo.	I surf the Internet, I go for a walk/stroll.
¿Tocas algun instrumento?	Do you play any instruments?
Toco el piano/el violín/la batería.	I play the piano/the violin/the drums.
No toco ningún instrumento.	I don't play an instrument.
¿Qué opinas de (montar a caballo)?	What do you think about (horse riding)?
Me gusta (mucho), me encanta.	I like it (a lot), I love it.
No me gusta (mucho), (lo/la) odio.	I don't like it (very much), I hate (it).
¿Por qué? Porque es aburrido/divertido.	Why? Because it is boring/fun.

el alpinismo	mountain climbing	en bici	on a bike
el billar	billiards	en moto	on a motorbike
el ajedrez	chess	en patines	on skates
el windsurf	windsurfing	bailar, cantar	to dance, to sing
la lectura	reading	jugar (a)	to play
la natación	swimming	leer, nadar	to read, to swim
dar una vuelta	go out (for a ride)	pescar/ir de pesca	to go fishing
en monopatín	on a skateboard	participar, practicar	take part, practise

Remember
Use jugar for playing ball-games, and tocar for playing musical instruments.

D   Your home

¿Vives en una casa o en un piso?	Do you live in a house or a flat?
Vivo en (una casa) de (dos) plantas.	I live in a (house) with (two) floors.
¿Cuántas habitaciones tiene?	How many rooms has it got?
¿Cuáles son? Hay (una cocina ...)	What are they? There's (a kitchen ...)
Descríbeme tu dormitorio: ¿cómo es?	Describe your bedroom: what's it like?
Es grande/pequeño/mediano. Tiene ...	It's big/small/medium-sized. It's got ...

una casa adosada	a terraced house	una cama	a bed
una casa doble	a semi (-detached)	una mesilla	a bedside table
un chalé, una finca	a bungalow, a farm	un guardarropa	a wardrobe
una torre	a tower block	un pupitre	a desk
una entrada	a hall	una silla/butaca	a chair/armchair
un vestuario	a cloakroom	un tocador	a dressing-table
un salón	a living-room	un armario	a cupboard
un comedor	a dining-room	una alfombra	a rug
las escaleras	the stairs, staircase	un estéreo	a stereo
(tres) dormitorios	(three) bedrooms	un televisor	a TV set
un cuarto de baño	a bathroom	un ordenador	a computer

Remember
A small flat is un apartamento. Un piso is usually a larger flat.

A Nouns and articles

A noun can be a thing (e.g. *a bike*), a place (e.g. *a room*) or a person (e.g. *a man*).
A Spanish noun is either masculine *(m)* or feminine *(f)*.
Nouns can be singular *(s)* (one of them) or plural *(pl)* (more than one).

The words for 'the', 'a' and 'some' are as follows:

	masculine	*feminine*			*masculine*	*feminine*
(s)	**un** chico	**una** chica		(s)	**el** hermano	**la** hermana
	a boy	*a girl*			*the brother*	*the sister*
(pl)	**unos** chicos	**unas** chicas		(pl)	**los** hermanos	**las** hermanas
	some boys	*some girls*			*the brothers*	*the sisters*

B Plural nouns

Remember
Remember! If the singular ends in –z, this changes to –c in the plural: <u>lápiz</u> (pencil) – <u>lápices</u>.

Ending in a vowel (a, e, i, o, u), add an **–s** in the plural: see the examples above.
Ending in other consonants, add an **–es**: **ordenador** (computer) – **ordenador<u>es</u>**.
An accent on the final syllable in the singular disappears in the plural: **salón**, **sal<u>ones</u>**.
Words borrowed from other languages can also just add **-s**: **clubs**, **pósters**.

1 Put the following nouns in brackets into the plural. **Ejemplo:** cuatro dormitorios

a cuatro (dormitorio)   c dos (balcón)   e dos (garaje)
b dos (terraza)   d tres (pasillo)   f cuatro (televisor)

C Adjectives

Adjectives describe a noun, e.g. blue, tall, good-looking are all adjectives.
In Spanish, the ending of an adjective has to 'agree' with the noun it describes.
If the noun is feminine and/or plural, for example, so will the adjective be:

(ms)	*(fs)*	*(mpl)*	*(fpl)*		*(ms)*	*(fs)*	*(mpl)*	*(fpl)*
-o	-a	-os	-as		-ol	-ola	-oles	-olas
-a	-a	-as	-as		-or	-ora	-ores	-oras
-e	-e	-es	-es		-án	-ana	-anes	-anas
-és	-esa	-eses	-esas					

Other consonants: no change in *(fs)*, add **-es** for both *(mpl)* and *(fpl)*.
Marrón *(brown)*, **cortés** *(polite)*, **mayor/menor** *(older/younger)*: no change in the *(fs)*.
Lila *(lilac)*, **naranja** *(orange)* and **rosa** *(pink)* do not change at all.

2 Write the correct form of the adjective in Ana's description of herself and her family.
Ejemplo: Yo soy baja y de talla regular ...

Yo soy (bajo) y de talla regular, pero mi hermana (mayor) es (alto) y (delgado). Tengo los ojos (verde) y el pelo (marrón) y soy (cortés) y bastante (callado). Pero ella es (impaciente) y (hablador). ¿Mis hermanos (menor)? Son (inteligente) y (gracioso).

D Subject pronouns

Subject pronouns are the words which, in English, are: 'I', 'you', 'he', 'she', etc.
There are four words for 'you' in Spanish:

yo (I), **tú** (you, familiar), **él** (he), **ella** (she), **usted** (you, formal)

nosotros (we), **vosotros** (you, familiar), **ellos** (they, male), **ellas** (they, female), **ustedes** (you, formal)

E Regular present verbs

Remember
Familiar: use <u>tú</u> to people your age or younger, or an adult you know well. Formal: use <u>usted</u> to an adult you don't know well.

Spanish verbs end in **-ar**, **-er**, **-ir** in the infinitive form. The infinitive is the verb form which means 'to ...' in English: e.g. **hablar** means <u>to</u> speak, **comer** <u>to</u> eat, and **vivir** <u>to</u> live.

Below is the regular present tense. The present tense indicates what usually happens, or what happens at the moment, e.g. I go to school, I eat lunch at one, I live in Sheffield.

	hablar (to speak)	comer (to eat)	vivir (to live)
yo	hablo	como	vivo
tú	hablas	comes	vives
él, ella, usted	habla	come	vive
nosotros	hablamos	comemos	vivimos
vosotros	habláis	coméis	vivís
ellos, ellas, ustedes	hablan	comen	viven

F Irregular present tense verbs

These common verbs are only irregular in the **yo** (I) form.

dar (to give)	doy	saber (to know how to/a fact)	sé
conocer (to know a person/place)	conozco	salir (to go out, leave)	salgo
hacer (to do, make)	hago	traer (to bring)	traigo
poner (to put, set, lay)	pongo	ver (to see)	veo*

* Ver keeps an 'e' before the endings: veo, ves, ve, vemos, veis, ven

These common verbs are irregular. The six parts of each are as follows:

ir	(to go)	voy, vas, va, vamos, vais, van
estar	(to be)	estoy, estás, está, estamos, estáis, están
ser	(to be)	soy, eres, es, somos, sois, son
tener	(to have)	tengo, tienes, tiene, tenemos, tenéis, tienen

Remember
Use the verb <u>ser</u> when describing people, places or things, and use <u>estar</u> to indicate place, and temporary moods.

3 Write each verb in the dialogue below in its correct form. **Ejemplo:** 1 – conoces

1 Marta, ¿(conocer) a mi amiga Sharon? — Encantada. ¿De dónde (ser), Sharon?

2 Yo (vivir) en Edimburgo, en Escocia. — Sharon, ¿qué (hacer) aquí en España?

3 Mi hermano y yo (estar) de vacaciones. — ¿Cuántos años (tener) tu hermano?

4 Dieciocho años – y ¡(ser) muy guapo! — Y vosotros, ¿adónde (ir) esta tarde?

5 Yo no (saber) todavía. ¿Por qué? — Nosotros (salir) a la discoteca – ¿os interesa?

Self, family and friends

THE BARE BONES

➤ Conversations, forms and letters about yourself and your family feature frequently in the exam.

➤ Make sure you know the alphabet, the months of the year, and numbers 1–100.

A Personal details

SPEAK

1 You need to be able to answer questions about yourself and spell your name.

2 Read the conversation below. Study the sports club register (Club de Deportes).

3 Cambia las palabras subrayadas. Inventa cuatro conversaciones más.

Change the underlined words. Invent four more conversations.

– ¿Cómo te llamas?

+ Me llamo Marta.

– ¿Cuál es tu apellido?

+ Es Duarte.

– ¿Cómo se escribe?

+ D-U-A-R-T-E.

– ¿Cuántos años tienes?

+ Tengo quince años.

– ¿Cuándo es tu cumpleaños?

+ Es el uno de febrero.

CLUB DE DEPORTES

	Apellido	Nombre	Edad	Cumpleaños
1	Duarte	Marta	15	1/2
2	Elizalde	Curro	14	29/8
3	Gallego	Javier	17	15/4
4	Moreno	Zohora	13	20/7
5	Tejero	Nuria	16	3/11

B Describing yourself

WRITE

1 You may be asked to describe your build, hair and eyes. Use the dictionary to look up any words below which you don't know.

2 ¿Cómo eres? Describe tu físico. Describe what you look like.

(Height) (Shape)	Soy	alto(a)/bajo(a)/de estatura media.
		delgado(a)/fuerte/gordito(a).
(Hair colour) (Hair length) (Hair texture)	Tengo el pelo	marrón/rubio/negro.
		corto/largo/hasta el hombro.
		rizado/liso/ondulado.
(Eyes)	Tengo los ojos	marrones/verdes/grises/azules.
	Llevo	gafas/lentillas.

Remember
Adjectives ending in **-o** in the masculine form have **-a** in the feminine; those ending in **-e** remain the same.

C Family and friends

READ

KEY FACT

1 In the next activity, you have to match the paragraphs A-G of the letter to the correct topics. There will be one left over.

> Look for the words you know. What clues do they give you?

Q What information are you asked to include when you reply?

2 <u>Escribe la letra en cada casilla. No se necesitan todas las letras.</u>

Write the letter in each box. You do not need all the letters.

1 Name ☐

A Mi cumpleaños es el doce de junio. ¿Y tú? ¿Cuándo es tu cumpleaños?

2 Age ☐

B Me gusta mucho mi perro, que es negro y marrón - ¡es mi mejor amigo!

3 Birthday ☐

C ¡Hola! Me llamo Iñigo Bernal Arroyos.

4 Nationality ☐

D Mi padre no vive aquí con mi madre - están separados.

5 Brothers/sisters ☐

E Tengo una hermana, Nieves, pero no tengo hermanos.

6 Parents ☐

F Soy colombiano. Nací aqui en la capital.

G Tengo dieciséis años, y vivo con mi familia en las afueras. ¿Cuántas personas hay en tu familia?

PRACTICE

Read the information on the form below, and write a sentence for every heading.

Although you won't get marks for copying directly, you can adapt the Spanish on the exam paper. Here, you could reuse <u>tengo</u>, <u>vivo</u>, <u>me llamo</u>, <u>mi cumpleaños es</u> ...

I	Nombre y Apellido:	Ana Gómez
2	Nacionalidad:	española
3	Lugar de nacimiento:	Granada
4	Fecha de nacimiento:	23.7.1988
5	Familia:	I hermano (Pablo), padres divorciados
6	Animales:	gato (gris, blanco)

THE BARE BONES

> ➤ You need to be able to talk about how you spend your free time.
> ➤ Giving your opinion, likes and dislikes is also important.

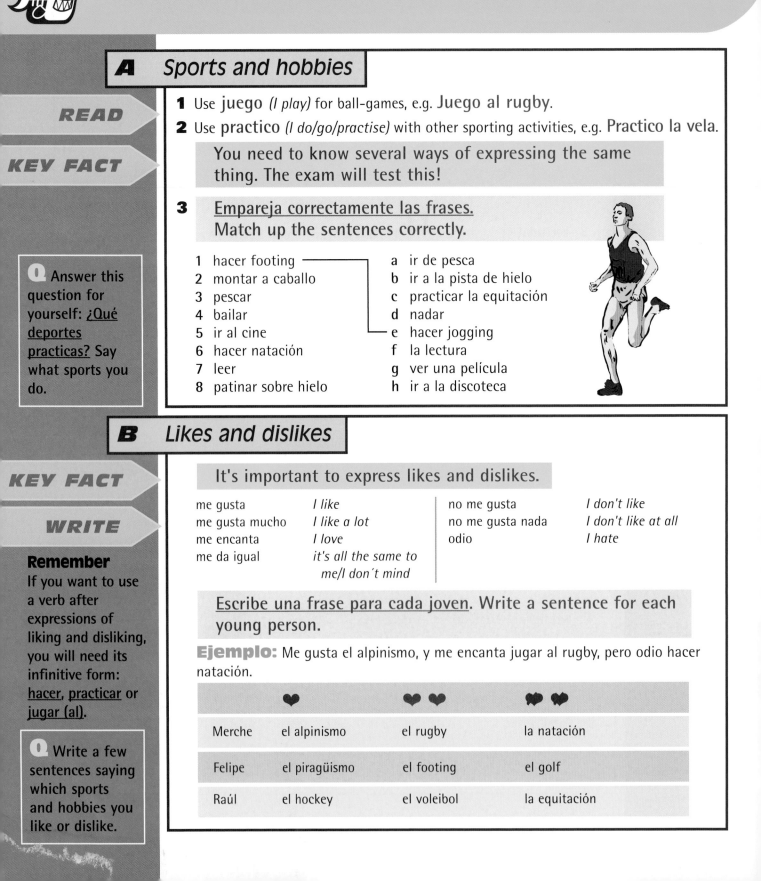

A Sports and hobbies

READ

1 Use **juego** *(I play)* for ball-games, e.g. Juego al rugby.

2 Use **practico** *(I do/go/practise)* with other sporting activities, e.g. Practico la vela.

KEY FACT

You need to know several ways of expressing the same thing. The exam will test this!

3 Empareja correctamente las frases.
Match up the sentences correctly.

1	hacer footing	a ir de pesca
2	montar a caballo	b ir a la pista de hielo
3	pescar	c practicar la equitación
4	bailar	d nadar
5	ir al cine	e hacer jogging
6	hacer natación	f la lectura
7	leer	g ver una película
8	patinar sobre hielo	h ir a la discoteca

Q Answer this question for yourself: **¿Qué deportes practicas?** Say what sports you do.

B Likes and dislikes

KEY FACT

WRITE

It's important to express likes and dislikes.

me gusta	*I like*	no me gusta	*I don't like*
me gusta mucho	*I like a lot*	no me gusta nada	*I don't like at all*
me encanta	*I love*	odio	*I hate*
me da igual	*it's all the same to me/I don´t mind*		

Remember
If you want to use a verb after expressions of liking and disliking, you will need its infinitive form: **hacer**, **practicar** or **jugar (al)**.

Escribe una frase para cada joven. Write a sentence for each young person.

Ejemplo: Me gusta el alpinismo, y me encanta jugar al rugby, pero odio hacer natación.

	❤	❤ ❤	❤ ❤
Merche	el alpinismo	el rugby	la natación
Felipe	el piragüismo	el footing	el golf
Raúl	el hockey	el voleibol	la equitación

Q Write a few sentences saying which sports and hobbies you like or dislike.

C Giving reasons

Q Your teacher will ask you why (¿por qué?) you like your leisure activities. Prepare your reply. Begin: <u>Porque</u> ... (Because)

Make sure you can say why you like or dislike a sport or hobby.

Learn the phrases below to help. They will be useful in other topics too.

Es ...	It's ...	gratis	free
divertido/a	fun	peligroso/a	dangerous
aburrido/a	boring	relajante	relaxing
caro/a	expensive	un deporte individual	an individual sport
barato/a	cheap	un deporte de equipo	a team sport

D Saying when and how often

Earn more marks by adding detail about when and how often.

- Mention which **days of the week** you do a hobby or sport.
- Talk about the different activities you do in **winter and summer.**

<u>Escribe en español las frases en inglés.</u>
Write the English phrases in Spanish.

1 en primavera (*in spring*) in summer, in autumn, in winter
2 en enero (*in January*) in September
3 una vez por semana (*once a week*) once a month
4 dos veces por semana (*twice a week*) three times a week
5 los viernes por la noche (*on Friday nights*) on Monday nights
6 los jueves/domingos (*on Thursdays/Sundays*) on Tuesdays/Saturdays
7 el doce de mayo (*on 12th May*) on 16th June

Q Prepare a 60 to 90-second presentation on your leisure time.

Exam hint: In the presentation part of the exam, you may take in a few headings on cards to remind you what to say – but you may only write verbs in the infinitive form.

PRACTICE

Practise the following conversation. Then answer the four questions, so that they are true for you, in Spanish.

– ¿Qué te gusta hacer en tu tiempo libre?
+ ...(1)... me gusta jugar al baloncesto. Juego al fútbol y practico la natación ...(2)... .
– ¿Eres miembro de algún club?
+ Soy miembro del club de ordenadores. Nos reunimos ..(3)... .
– ¿Tocas algún instrumento?
+ El martes ...(4)... tengo clase de guitarra.
– ¿Qué haces el fin de semana?
+ ...(5)... salgo con mis amigos a la discoteca. Y hago mis deberes ...(6)... .

1 in winter
2 in July and August
3 twice a week
4 after school
5 on Friday nights
6 on Sundays

your home and bedroom

THE BARE BONES

➤ Understanding and giving information about your home is important.

➤ You also need to be able to describe your bedroom in detail.

A Your home

WRITE

> Describe your home as fully as you can.

1 Let's look at how to **improve your description** of your home.

2 Read the information about Miguel's home below.

> ¿Cuántos adjetivos tiene? How many adjectives does it have?

Vivo en una casa[1] en las afueras de la ciudad. Tiene siete habitaciones: una entrada[2], una cocina[3], un salón-comedor[4], un cuarto de baño y tres dormitorios. Hay una terraza[5] con flores. Delante de la casa no hay jardín, pero al lado hay un garaje. Detrás hay un cesped[7], y un patio[8] con una mesa y sillas.

It doesn't contain any adjectives at all! Let's improve it by **adding some adjectives**.

3 Use each of the adjectives 1–8 below after each of the nouns 1–8 in his letter.

Ejemplo: Vivo en una casa antigua ...

Remember
If the noun is feminine (una), then the adjectives which go with it must be feminine as well.

1 antiguo/a *(old)*
2 pequeño/a *(small)*
3 amueblado/a *(fitted)*
4 grande *(big)*

5 espacioso/a *(spacious)*
6 bonito/a *(pretty)*
7 verde *(green)*
8 nuevo/a *(new)*

B Adding detail

READ

1 Miguel doesn't explain where things are. Include **extra details for interest**.

2 Match up the Spanish and English phrases below.

Q Think about the layout of your own home. Write a few sentences explaining where rooms are, and which floor they're on.

1 a la izquierda
2 a la derecha
3 al fondo
4 en la planta baja
5 en el primer piso
6 arriba
7 abajo
8 que da a la terraza
9 en total

a *downstairs*
b *which opens onto the terrace*
c *on the first floor*
d *upstairs*
e *on the left*
f *altogether/in total*
g *on the ground floor*
h *at the end/back/rear*
i *on the right*

C Your bedroom

Preparation is the key to doing well in the conversation part of the exam.

1 You may well be asked to **describe your bedroom** in the speaking test.

2 In the writing exam, you may be asked to **list six or more things** which are in it.

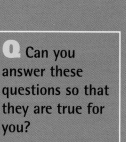

Q Look around your own room. Name each thing in it in Spanish. Use your notes or the dictionary to add at least another five which don't appear in the puzzle. Begin: Hay ... (There is ...). Don't forget you will need the Spanish for 'a': (un/una) in front of each.

Q Can you answer these questions so that they are true for you?

Completa el rompecabezas.
Complete the puzzle by writing in the vowels (a, e, i, o, u)

1 You sleep in this!

2 Useful for hanging things in.

3 A floor is cold without this.

4 Good for putting books on.

5 Every room has at least one!

6 Useful to have beside the bed.

7 Should have plenty of drawers.

8 You can puts lots of things in it

Crossword letters shown:
1: c _ _ m _
2: g _ _ _ r d _ _ r r _ _ p _
3: _ l f _ _ m b r _
4: _ s t _ n t _
5: p _ _ _ r t _
6: m _ s _ _ l l _
7: c _ m _ d _
8: (down)

Make sure to prepare your replies to common questions on this topic.

Rellena los huecos. Complete the gaps.

¿Tienes tu propio dormitorio?
No, lo tengo que ...(1)... con mi hermano.
¿Cómo es tu dormitorio?
Es ...(2)... pequeño, y empapelado y pintado en ...(3)... .
¿Qué hay en tu dormitorio?
Hay una cama, una mesilla de ...(4)... con una lámpara, un guardarropa, un ...(5)... para libros, un escritorio donde hago mis ...(6)..., y una silla.
¿Te gusta tu dormitorio?
Sí, porque es cómodo, y tengo muchos ...(7)... en las paredes.

noche	deberes	bastante	compartir	pósters	azul	estante

Write a detailed description of your home.
Include the following details:

- the type of housing you live in
- how many rooms it has, and where they are
- where it is in the town/village
- which rooms are on which floor
- if it has a garden and garage

You can reuse this description in the conversation part of the speaking test: make what you do work for you!

A Your town/village

¿Dónde vives? Vivo en (Newcastle).	*Where do you live? I live in Newcastle.*
¿Dónde está exactamente?	*Where is it exactly?*
Está en el (norte) de (Inglaterra).	*It's in the (north) of (England).*
¿Cuál es tu dirección?	*What's your address?*
La calle/avenida/plaza ..., número ...	*... street/avenue/square, number ...*
Vivo en las afueras, en el centro	*I live in the outskirts, in the centre*
en la sierra, en la costa, junto a un río	*in the mountains, on the coast, by a river*
en una urbanización, en el barrio de ...	*on a housing estate, in the area of ...*

hay ...	*there is/are ...*	un centro comercial	*a shopping centre*
colegios/institutos	*schools*	una pista de hielo	*an ice-rink*
bares, tiendas	*bars, shops*	una bolera	*a bowling alley*
restaurantes	*restaurants*	una piscina	*a pool*
un polideportivo	*a sports centre*	un teatro	*a theatre*
un cine	*a cinema*	una estación	*a station*

Remember
A railway station can either be <u>una estación de trenes</u>, or <u>una estación de ferrocarriles</u>.

B School subjects, likes and dislikes

¿Qué asignaturas estudias?	*How many subjects do you study?*
Estudio (siete) en total.	*I study (seven) altogether.*
(Cinco) obligatorias, y (dos) optativas.	*(Five) compulsory, and (two) options.*
¿Cuáles son? Estudio (la física ...)	*What are they? I study (physics ...)*
¿Qué asignatura te gusta más/menos?	*Which subject do you like best/least?*
¿Por qué te gusta/no te gusta?	*Why do you like it/not like it?*
¿Cómo es tu instituto?	*What's your school like?*
¿Qué instalaciones tiene?	*What facilities does it have?*

la lengua	*(English) language*	las ciencias	*sciences*
la literatura	*literature*	la química	*chemistry*
el francés	*French*	la biología	*biology*
el alemán	*German*	la ética	*PSHE*
el español	*Spanish*	el arte dramático	*drama*
la geografía	*geography*	el comercio	*business studies*
la historia	*history*	el dibujo, el diseño	*art, design*
la informática	*IT, computing*	las matemáticas	*maths*
la tecnología	*technology*	los trabajos manuales	*CDT*

(no) me gusta(n)	*I (don't) like*	saco buenas/malas notas	*I get good/bad marks*
me encanta(n)	*I love*		
odio, detesto	*I hate*	laboratorios, pasillos	*labs, corridors*
porque	*because*	aulas	*classrooms*
es (interesante)	*it's (interesting)*	una cantina	*a canteen*
útil, fácil, difícil	*useful, easy, hard*	un patio	*a playground*

Remember
Learn the gender and number (masculine, feminine, singular or plural) of each subject in Spanish. You will need to know this when you add an adjective, e.g. <u>las matemáticas son divertidas</u>.

C The immediate future

To indicate the immediate future – what is going to happen – use the verb ir *(to go)* followed by **a** and the infinitive of another verb:

yo	**voy**	*I go*	nosotros	**vamos**	*we go*
tú	**vas**	*you go*	vosotros	**vais**	*you go*
él	**va**	*he goes*	ellos	**van**	*they go*
ella	**va**	*she goes*	ellas	**van**	*they go*
usted	**va**	*you go*	ustedes	**van**	*you go*

Voy a estudiar francés.	*I'm going to study French.*
¿Qué vas a hacer en septiembre?	*What are you going to do in September?*
Vamos a salir a las ocho.	*We're going to leave at eight o'clock.*

Remember
Voy a ..., vas a ..., etc. can also be followed by ir:
voy a ir a España. (I'm going to go to Spain.)

D Gustar (to like, be pleasing to)

Gustar means 'to be pleasing to', translated in English as 'to like'.
With singular nouns (**el, la**), use **gusta**. With plural nouns (**los, las**) use **gustan**.

Me gusta el inglés.	*I like English. (To me is pleasing English.)*
Me gusta la informática.	*I like IT. (To me is pleasing IT.)*
Me gustan los trabajos manuales.	*I like CDT. (To me is pleasing CDT.)*
Me gustan las matemáticas.	*I like maths. (To me is pleasing maths.)*

Before **gustar**, you need an indirect object pronoun.

E Indirect object pronouns

(yo)	**me**	*to me*	(nosotros)	**nos**	*to us*
(tú)	**te**	*to you*	(vosotros)	**os**	*to you*
(él, ella, usted)	**le**	*to him, her, you*	(ellos, ellas, ustedes)	**les**	*to them, to you*

¿Te gusta la historia?	*Do you like history?*
A Felipe, le gusta la ética.	*Felipe likes PSHE.*
¡No nos gustan los deberes!	*We don't like homework!*

F Reflexive verbs

Reflexive verbs indicate an action done to oneself (e.g. washing oneself, getting oneself up) and you will notice that they have a pronoun (**me, te**, etc.) in front.

yo	**me lavo**	*I wash*	nosotros	**nos lavamos**	*we wash*
tú	**te lavas**	*you wash*	vosotros	**os laváis**	*you wash*
él	**se lava**	*he washes*	ellos	**se lavan**	*they wash*
ella	**se lava**	*she washes*	ellas	**se lavan**	*they wash*
usted	**se lava**	*you wash*	ustedes	**se lavan**	*you wash*

Me lavo o me ducho todos los dias.	*I wash or have a shower everyday.*
¿A qué hora te levantas?	*What time do you get up?*

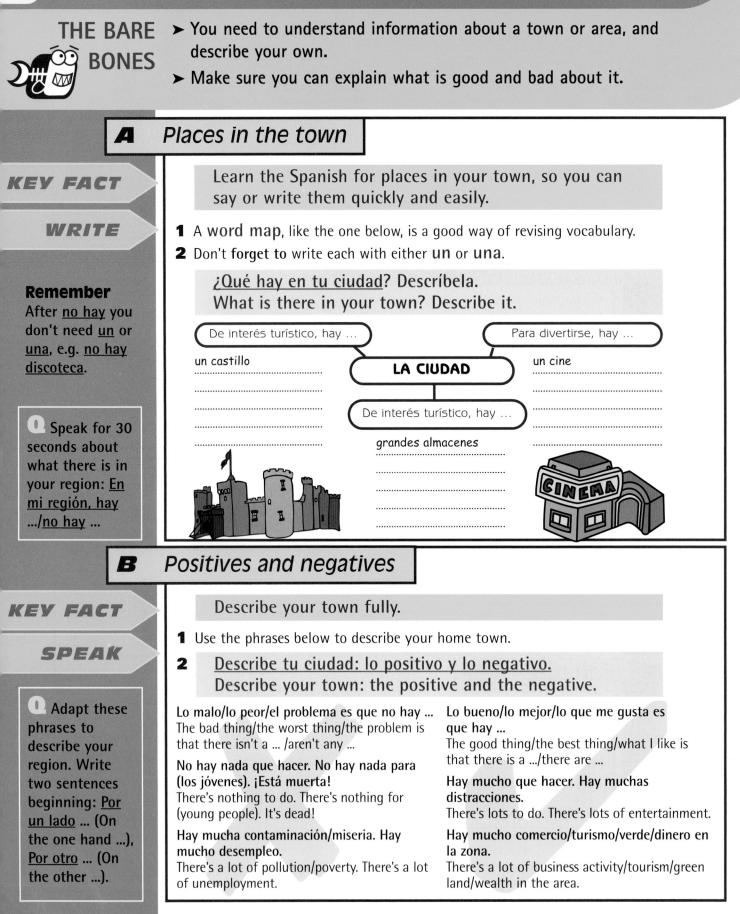

> ➤ You need to understand information about a town or area, and describe your own.
> ➤ Make sure you can explain what is good and bad about it.

A Places in the town

KEY FACT

Learn the Spanish for places in your town, so you can say or write them quickly and easily.

WRITE

1 A **word map**, like the one below, is a good way of revising vocabulary.
2 Don't **forget to** write each with either **un** or **una**.

¿Qué hay en tu ciudad? Descríbela.
What is there in your town? Describe it.

Remember
After no hay you don't need un or una, e.g. no hay discoteca.

De interés turístico, hay ...

un castillo
....
....
....
....

LA CIUDAD

De interés turístico, hay ...

grandes almacenes
....
....
....
....

Para divertirse, hay ...

un cine
....
....
....
....

Q Speak for 30 seconds about what there is in your region: En mi región, hay .../no hay ...

B Positives and negatives

KEY FACT

Describe your town fully.

SPEAK

1 Use the phrases below to describe your home town.
2 Describe tu ciudad: lo positivo y lo negativo.
   Describe your town: the positive and the negative.

Q Adapt these phrases to describe your region. Write two sentences beginning: Por un lado ... (On the one hand ...), Por otro ... (On the other ...).

Lo malo/lo peor/el problema es que no hay ...
The bad thing/the worst thing/the problem is that there isn't a ... /aren't any ...

No hay nada que hacer. No hay nada para (los jóvenes). ¡Está muerta!
There's nothing to do. There's nothing for (young people). It's dead!

Hay mucha contaminación/miseria. Hay mucho desempleo.
There's a lot of pollution/poverty. There's a lot of unemployment.

Lo bueno/lo mejor/lo que me gusta es que hay ...
The good thing/the best thing/what I like is that there is a .../there are ...

Hay mucho que hacer. Hay muchas distracciones.
There's lots to do. There's lots of entertainment.

Hay mucho comercio/turismo/verde/dinero en la zona.
There's a lot of business activity/tourism/green land/wealth in the area.

C *Understanding descriptions*

READ

1 A common exam question type asks you to **decide which statements on a text are true, false,** or **whether the text does not say.**

2 Read the questions through first **so you know what you're looking for.**

3 **Watch out for negatives,** because these change the sense.

4 **Read for meaning,** rather than trying to spot the same words as in the questions.

Ejemplo: **Pobre** (*poor*) means the same as **no tiene dinero** (*doesn't have any money*).

Remember
Negatives make a difference to the meaning! Learn these: <u>no</u> ... nunca/jamás (never), <u>no</u> ... nada (nothing), <u>no</u> ... <u>nadie</u> (no-one).

Q Speak for 30 seconds about what there is in your region: <u>En mi región, hay ...</u>/<u>no hay ...</u>

Q How would you reply to the questions: <u>¿Dónde vives?</u> <u>¿Cómo es tu ciudad?</u> <u>¿Qué hay como distracciones?</u> <u>¿Te gusta tu región?</u>

Lee la carta de Santi. Para cada afirmación 1–9, escribe verdad (V), mentira (M) o no dice (ND).
Read the letter from Santi. For each statement 1–9, write true (V), false (M) or doesn't say (ND).

1 Santi vive en el sur de su país. _____ .

2 Hay mucho para los turistas en la ciudad. _____ .

3 No hay muchas distracciones para los jóvenes en el centro. _____ .

4 A Santi le gusta mucho su ciudad. _____ .

5 La ciudad está en la costa. _____ .

6 No hay mucho verde. _____ .

7 Todo el mundo tiene empleo. _____ .

8 El tráfico es un problema en el centro. _____ .

9 La vida en los pueblos es aburrida para los jóvenes. _____ .

¡Hola! Me llamo Santi y vivo en el norte de Colombia. Mi ciudad se llama Cartagena. De interés turístico, hay la parte antigua, la catedral y el Palacio de la Inquisición. Para comprar, hay las tiendas turísticas y un mercado. Para divertirse, hay la playa, la fiesta (en marzo) y muchos clubs y discotecas, y un cine. Pero si te gustan las distracciones, hay que tener dinero – ¡y nadie lo tiene! ¿Cómo es mi ciudad? Es histórica y bonita, pero también ruidosa y un poco sucia. ¿Y la región? Por un lado hay mucho turismo y mucho comercio; por otro, en algunas zonas hay mucho desempleo. Lo bueno es que hay mucho campo bonito, pero el problema es que no hay mucho para los jóvenes en los pueblos.

You may not need to count the number of words you write in the exam. The examiner will be looking for quality of writing, not length. Check what your exam board says about this.

PRACTICE

Try writing a description of your own home town or village and area. Re-read Santi's letter and use it as a basis for your own.

Daily routine

THE BARE BONES
➤ Talk about your routine during the weekend, and at weekends.
➤ Discuss mealtimes at home and school, and food preferences.

A Daily routine

KEY FACT

> Reflexive verbs are very important here: **me levanto, me visto ...**, etc.

SPEAK

1 Make sure you revise **question words** thoroughly:

¿cuando? *(when?)*; ¿quién? *(who?)*; ¿dónde? *(where?)*; ¿qué? *(what?)*; ¿cómo? *(how?)*; ¿cuál? *(which?)*; ¿por qué? *(why?)*; ¿adónde? *(where ... to?)*; ¿cuánto? *(how much?)*; ¿a qué hora? *(at what time?)*.

2 Read the questions below and work out **the appropriate question word in Spanish** for numbers 1, 3, 5, 7, 9, 11, 13, 15.

3 Answer each question so it is true for you. **Begin each answer with the verb in brackets.**

> <u>Contesta a estas preguntas en español.</u>
> Answer these questions in Spanish.

1 ¿(*At what time*) te levantas?　　　　　(Me levanto …)
2 ¿Qué llevas para ir al instituto?　　　　(Llevo …)
3 ¿(*How*) vas al instituto?　　　　　　　(Voy …)
4 ¿A qué hora sales de casa?　　　　　　(Salgo …)
5 ¿(*How much*) tiempo tardas en llegar?　(Tardo …)
6 ¿A qué hora empiezan las clases?　　　　(Empiezan …)
7 ¿(*How many*) clases hay por día?　　　　(Hay …)
8 ¿Cuánto tiempo dura cada clase?　　　　(Las clases duran …)
9 ¿(*When*) hay recreos?　　　　　　　　(Hay recreos …)
10 ¿A qué hora terminan las clases?　　　　(Terminan …)
11 ¿(*Where*) comes al mediodía?　　　　　(Como …)
12 ¿Cuándo vuelves a casa?　　　　　　　(Vuelvo …)
13 ¿(*How many*) horas de deberes haces?　(Hago …)
14 ¿Qué te gusta hacer por la tarde?　　　　(Me gusta …)
15 ¿(*At what time*) te acuestas?　　　　　(Me acuesto a …)

4 How is your routine different at the weekend? Write a paragraph explaining when you get up, what you do during the day, and when you go to bed. Look back at 'Interests and Hobbies' on pages 14–15.

Remember
The question word <u>cuánto</u> is an adjective, and so it has to agree with the noun it describes, e.g.
<u>¿Cuántos años tienes?</u>
<u>¿Cuántas horas de clase tienes al día?</u>

Q How many question words can you list in two minutes?

B Mealtimes

READ

1 You will need to explain **when, where and with whom** you have your meals.

> **¿Cada persona habla o de la mañana (M), o del mediodía (D) o de la tarde (T)?**
> Is each person talking about the morning (M), midday (D) or evening (T)?

> No tengo hambre. No desayuno mucho: cereales con leche, y un café.
> *Dani*

> Suelo tomar tostadas, y un zumo de fruta. ¡No tengo mucho tiempo para desayunar más!
> *Paco*

> Almuerzo en el instituto con mis amigos. Voy a la cantina, y tomo un bocadillo o una pizza.
> *Alicia*

> El fin de semana, comemos sobre la una y media: dos o tres platos y un postre.
> *Lorenzo*

> A veces, ceno delante de la tele con mi hermano, pero en general ceno con mi familia en el comedor.
> *Nuria*

Remember
<u>Como</u> means both 'I eat' and 'I have lunch'. Similarly, <u>la comida</u> can mean both 'lunch' and 'food'.

2 Which foods do you like or dislike, or not eat? Read Ben's account below, and find five expressions for liking, disliking, or preferring.

> Learn as many ways of expressing likes and dislikes as you can. They will be useful in many different topic areas.

KEY FACT

¡Hola, me llamo Ben! ¿Qué tipo de comida me gusta? Pues, ¡varios! Me gustan las pastas – macarrones, espaguettis, lasaña – en salsa de tomate con queso. Pero no tomo ni pescado ni carne. Me encantan los huevos también, pero lo que más me gusta es la tortilla española. Las verduras y las ensaladas son muy buenas también. Pero odio el colifor: es algo que no aguanto. En cuanto a bebidas, prefiero el zumo de fruta – pero no bebo café.

Q Use the key words <u>desayuno, almuerzo, ceno</u> to describe when and where you have meals.

PRACTICE

Read Ben's description again, and complete the form.

Nombre: _____

Comida preferida: _____

Detesta: _____

Le gusta beber: _____

¿Vegetariano/a? (dibuja un círculo) Sí/No

> Read forms carefully in the exam, and write down only the information you're asked for. Here for example, <u>comida preferida</u> means the food he prefers above all others, not just any foods he likes.

THE BARE BONES
➤ Make sure you can say which subjects you study.
➤ Add your opinions, likes and dislikes about school.
➤ Explain what you're going to do after the exams.

A   Likes and dislikes

KEY FACT

Check that you know different ways of expressing likes and dislikes: look again at page 18.

READ

1 A common exam question type asks you **to read a short passage**, and then **tick the sentences about it which are true.**

2 **Do not assume** that all expressions of **disliking** or **not liking** have **no** in them. You can use **no me gusta nada** (*I don't like*), but also **odio/detesto** (*I hate*).

Escribe ✓ en las casillas si las frases son verdaderas.
Put a ✓ in the boxes beside the sentences below which are true.

Remember
English, as a subject, is called 'lengua y literatura' if it is your own language. Only say estudio inglés (I study English) if English is a foreign language for you.

> ¡Hola!
>
> Me llamo Nuria. Mi colegio es grande: tiene más de mil alumnos. Es bastante nuevo, con muchas aulas, pasillos, laboratorios, un gimnasio, un salón de actos, una biblioteca, despachos para la administración y el director, dos cocinas, un patio y una cantina. Mi asignatura favorita es el deporte, pero se me dan muy bien las ciencias también. No me gusta nada el inglés ni el francés, porque son difíciles y aburridos; y odio la historia porque no saco nunca buenas notas. En general, no está mal mi instituto. Lo bueno es que tengo muchos amigos y los profesores son simpáticos.

Remember
You need to learn the following negatives: no ... nada (nothing, not anything), ni ... ni ... (neither ... nor), and no ... nunca (never)

1 El instituto de Nuria es pequeña. ☐

2 Su instituto no es muy antiguo. ☐

3 Le encanta hacer deporte. ☐

4 Le gusta mucho estudiar la física, la química y la biología. ☐

5 Las lenguas no le interesan mucho. ☐

6 Nuria saca buenas notas en historia. ☐

7 Nuria está bastante contenta de su instituto. ☐

B After the exams

Make sure you can use the simple future tense: voy a ...
(I'm going to ...)

1 You will need to prepare a few sentences on **your plans for after the exams.**

2 Use the grid below to do the role-play task. **Put the English sentences into Spanish.**

You are talking to your Spanish friend about your plans for the rest of the year.

¿Qué vas a hacer después de los exámenes?
(Say you're going to have a rest!)
¿Vas a quedarte en casa todo el verano?
(Say you'd also like to look for a job and earn some money.)
¿Y en septiembre?
(Explain that you're going to return to school and carry on studying.)
¿Vas a hacer más exámenes?
(Tell him/her that you hope to do do A-levels.)

Remember
The Spanish exam COU (Curso de Orientación Universitaria) is the nearest equivalent to our A/S and A-level exams.

Después de los exámenes, quiero ...	descansar un rato.
En verano, me gustaría .../voy a ...	ir de vacaciones.
	trabajar en mi ciudad.
	ganar dinero.
	pasarlo bien.
En septiembre, voy a ...	volver al instituto.
En el otoño, espero ...	cambiar de instituto.
	seguir estudiando.
	hacer el COU.
	buscar un empleo.

Q How would you answer the questions so they are true for you?

PRACTICE

Write at least one sentence on each of the following themes:

• las asignaturas que estudias
• la asignatura que te gusta más, y por qué
• una asignatura que no te gusta, y por qué
• tu colegio: lo bueno y lo malo
• qué vas a hacer depués de los exámenes

Vocabulary and phrases you've used in one topic can be reused in another. Look back at pages 14–15 for more expressions of liking/disliking, pages 16–17 for adjectives to describe your school, and pages 20–21 to say what is good and bad about it.

Vocabulary

A Asking the way

Remember
Todo derecho is an alternative to todo recto (straight ahead). Take care not to confuse it with derecha (right).

¿Hay (un bar/una farmacia) por aquí?	Is there (a bar/a chemist's) near here?
Sí, hay (uno/una) en ...	Yes, there's (one) in ...
¿Por dónde se va a ...? ¿Para ir a ...?	How do you get to ...?
Tome/coge, tuerza, cruce	Take, turn, cross
la primera/segunda/tercera (calle)	the first/second/third (street)
a la izquierda, a la derecha	on the left, on the right
Siga todo recto (hasta ...)	Carry straight on (as far as ...)
Está/están ...	It is/they are ...
delante (de), detrás (de), enfrente (de),	in front (of), behind, opposite,
al lado (de), encima (de), debajo (de),	beside, on top (of), underneath/below,
entre, cerca (de), lejos (de)	between, near (to), far (from)

Remember
If you want to buy medicine, antibiotics, etc. you need la farmacia. La droguería sells toiletries and cleaning products.

la calle	the street	un aparcamiento	a car park
la avenida	the avenue	un banco	a bank
la plaza	the square	un castillo	a castle
la autopista	the motorway	una comisaría	a police station
la carretera	the road	una iglesia	a church
el cruce	the crossroads	un monumento	a monument
el semáforo	the traffic lights	el Ayuntamiento	the Town Hall

un mercado	a market	una carnicería	a butcher's
un estanco	a tobacconist's	una pescadería	a fishmonger's
un quiosco	a kiosk, stall	una cafetería	a café
un supermercado	a supermarket	una tabacalería	a tobacconist's
una panadería	a baker's	una confitería	a sweetshop
una pastelería	a cake shop	una droguería	a toiletries shop
una frutería	a greengrocer's	una zapatería	a shoe shop

B Travel and transport

Quisiera/quiero comprar/sacar ...	I'd like to/I want to buy/get ...
un billete de ida/un billete sencillo	a single ticket
un billete de ida y vuelta (para)	a return ticket (to)
un billete de primera/segunda clase	first/standard class ticket
fumador, no fumador	smoking, non-smoking
un bonobús	a book of bus tickets
¿A qué hora llega (el tren de ...)?	When does (the train from ...) arrive?
¿A qué hora sale (el autocar para ...)?	When does (the coach for ...) leave?
¿De qué andén sale?	What platform does it leave from?
¿Hay que cambiar/hacer transbordo?	Do you have to change?
¿Cuánto tiempo tarda en llegar?	How long does it take to get there?
¿Hay que pagar un suplemento?	Do you have to pay a supplement?

un aeropuerto	an airport	un viajero	the traveller
un avión, un barco	a plane, a boat	un pasajero	the passenger
el metro	the underground	un andén	the platform
un aerodeslizador	a hovercraft	una consigna	a left-luggage office
el AVE, el Talgo	the national	una sala de espera	a waiting room
	high-speed train	una taquilla	a ticket office
RENFE	Spanish Railways	las llegadas	arrivals
un coche	a car	las salidas	departures
un camión	a lorry	un vuelo	a flight
un conductor	a driver, motorist	una vía	a track
un revisor	a ticket collector		

C Weather

¿Qué tiempo hace?	What's the weather like?
Hace bueno, hace buen tiempo.	The weather is good/fine.
Hace malo, hace mal tiempo.	The weather's bad.
¿Qué dice el pronóstico?	What does the forecast say?
Hace/hará ...	It is/it will be ...
Hay/habrá ...	There is/there will be ...

hace frío	it's cold	hay hielo, granizo	there's ice, hail
hace calor	it's hot	hay tormenta	there's a storm
hace (mucho) sol	it's (very) sunny	el cielo está ...	the sky is ...
hace viento	it's windy	despejado	clear
hay lluvia, llueve	it's raining	nublado	cloudy
hay nieve, nieva	it's snowing	temperaturas altas	high temperatures
hay niebla/neblina	there's fog/mist	temperaturas bajas	low temperatures

D Tourism

¿Cómo es el pueblo/la ciudad?	What's the village town like?
¿Qué hay en el barrio?	What is there in the neighbourhood?
¿Qué se puede hacer?	What can you do?
Se puede (acampar, visitar, explorar ...)	You can (camp, visit, explore ...)
¿Dónde está la Oficina de Turismo?	Where is the Tourist Office?
Estoy/estamos aquí de vacaciones.	I am/we are here on holiday.
¿El restaurante está climatizada?	Is the restaurant air-conditioned?

un mapa	a map	alquilar	to hire
un plano	a town-plan	bañarse en el mar	to bathe in the sea
un folleto (sobre)	a brochure (about)	tomar el sol	to sunbathe
una guía turística	a tourist guide	divertirse	to enjoy oneself
un horario (de)	a timetable (of)	pasarlo bien	to have a good time
una lista (de)	a list (of)	descansar	to rest
un hotel	a hotel	sacar fotos	to take photos
una pensión	bed-and-breakfast	hacer turismo	to sightsee
un camping	a campsite	salir por la noche	to go out at night
un albergue juvenil	a youth hostel	ir de excursión	to take a trip

Remember
Use bastante to indicate 'quite': hace bastante bueno (the weather's quite good). Use mucho to indicate 'very': hace mucho calor (it's very hot).

Remember
For 'city', use una ciudad grande. Un pueblo can be a small town as well as a larger village. For a small village or hamlet, use una aldea.

Grammar

A Asking questions

English often uses 'do/does/don't' when asking questions.
You do not need it in Spanish – just put question marks round the sentence.

¿Quieres ir de excursión?	Do you want to go on a trip?
¿No quieres salir?	Don't you want to go out?

You can also use a question word:

¿dónde?	where?	¿cómo?	how?	¿quién(es)?	who?
¿adónde?	where to?	¿qué?	what?	¿de quién?	whose?
¿cuánto?	how much?	¿cuándo?	when?	¿por qué?	why?

¿Cuánto? is an adjective, so it agrees with the noun which follows it.

¡Cuánta gente en la playa!	What a lot of people on the beach!
¿Cuántos billetes quiere?	How many tickets do you want?
¿Cuántas personas vienen?	How many people are coming?

Remember
Cuál means 'which ...?', e.g. ¿Cuál es el tren para Madrid? (Which is the train for Madrid?). It also has a plural form, cuáles, e.g. ¿Cuáles son los alumnos ingleses? (Which are the English pupils?)

B A and De

A means 'to', and indicates 'away'. When followed by **el** it becomes **al**.

Voy a Madrid.	I'm going to Madrid.
¿A qué distancia está?	How far away is it?
Está a cien kilómetros.	It's a hundred kilometres away.
¿Vienes al bar?	Are you coming to the bar?

De means 'of'/'from'. When followed by **el** it becomes **del**.

Mi padre es de Granada.	My father is from Granada.
Un paquete de bombones.	A packet of sweets.
Está delante del cine.	It's in front of the cinema.

Remember
De also indicates possession: es el boli de mi amigo (it's my friend's biro – the biro of my friend).

1 Match up the halves of the sentences correctly. **Ejemplo:** 1–c

1	¿Por dónde se va al _____	a ... Madrid.
2	La cafetería está enfrente _____	b ... la panadería.
3	¿Felipe? Creo que es _____	c ... banco?
4	Perdone. ¿Para ir a los _____	d ... tiendas?
5	El estanco está detrás de _____	e ... farmacia, por favor?
6	Mañana, voy a ir a _____	f ... del mercado.
7	¿Por dónde se va a las _____	g ... de Murcia.
8	¿Cómo se va a la _____	h ... servicios?

C Positive commands

A positive command is an instruction to do something. Form them as follows:

-AR: **hablar** – *to speak*; -ER: **comer** – *to eat*; -IR: **escribir** – *to write*

TÚ	*go to the tú form of the present tense and remove the final –s:* habla(s) → habla, come(s) → come, escribe(s) → escribe
USTED	*go to the usted form of the present tense and alter the last letter:* habla → hable, come → coma, escribe → escriba

These verbs are irregular in some parts of their command form:

	cruzar *(to cross)*	torcer *(to turn)*	coger *(to take)*	seguir *(to carry on)*
TÚ	cruza	tuerce	coge	sigue
USTED	cruce	tuerza	coja	siga

D The perfect tense

The perfect tense indicates what has happened, e.g. 'I've lost ...' (my key); 'I've left my bag on the bus'; 'I've eaten seafood'. To form this tense, you will need two parts:

THE PERFECT TENSE				IRREGULARS	
-ar (dejar)	(yo) he	dejado	*I've left*	escrito hecho	*(written)* *(done)*
-er (comer)	(yo) he	comido	*I've eaten*	puesto muerto	*(put on)* *(died) (el/ella ha)*
-ir (salir)	(yo) he	salido	*I've left*	roto visto	*(broken)* *(seen)*

Remember
Use the perfect tense in Spanish in the same places as we use it in English: to indicate has/have (done, been, gone, etc.). The most common past tense is the preterite (see page 37).

Other forms you might need are:
- Tú has (dejado), etc. *You have (left)*, etc.
- Él, ella, usted ha (dejado), etc. *He/she has, you have (left)*, etc.

2 Work out the correct part of the verb in Spanish to go in the gaps below. The infinitive is in brackets.

Ejemplo: 1 ¿Has visitado el sur de España?

1 (visitar) ¿ _____ el sur de Espana? — *Have you visited the south of Spain?*

2 (perder) ¿_____ tu pasaporte? — *You've lost your passport?*

3 (probar) Sí, _____ la tortilla española. — *Yes, I've tried Spanish omelette.*

4 (salir) ¿Irene? _____ hace poco. — *Irene? She went out a little while ago.*

5 (dejar) Él _____ su dinero en casa. — *He has left his money at home.*

THE BARE BONES
- ➤ Make sure you understand simple notices and signs.
- ➤ Revise buying tickets, and asking for information.

A In the street

KEY FACT

READ

Learn names of shops and places in the town.

1 You need to **understand simple signs and notices** in the street and in shops.

2 The task below asks you to **match up each sign with the appropriate shop**.

3 This kind of task often has **one or more possibilities left over**.

4 Try the ones you know first. **Be careful** – there are two which mention 'estudiante'!

Escribe la letra correcta en cada casilla.
Write the correct letter in each box.

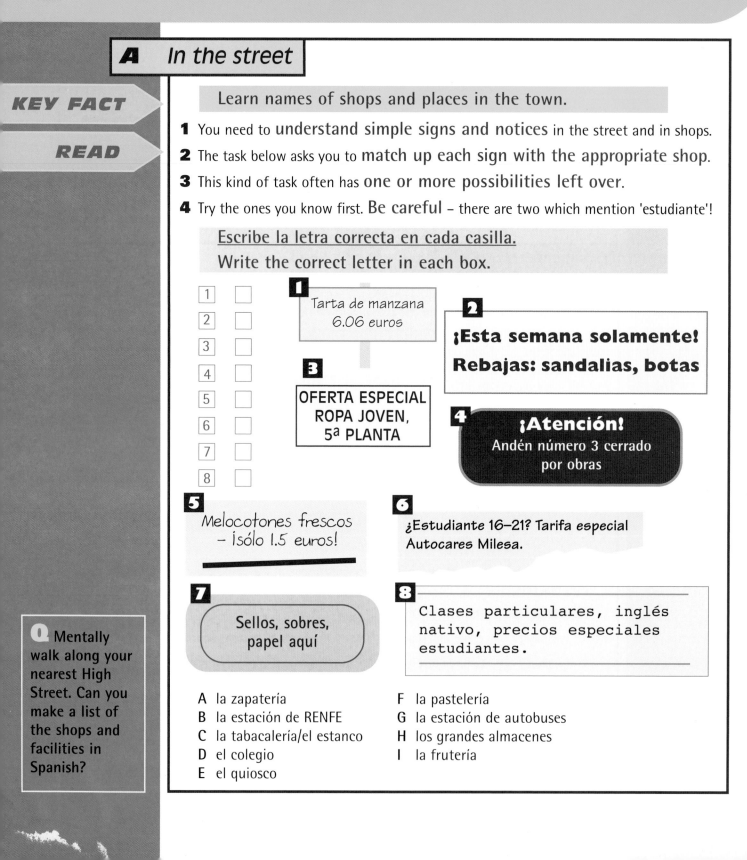

1 ☐
2 ☐
3 ☐
4 ☐
5 ☐
6 ☐
7 ☐
8 ☐

1
Tarta de manzana
6.06 euros

2
¡Esta semana solamente!
Rebajas: sandalias, botas

3
OFERTA ESPECIAL
ROPA JOVEN,
5ª PLANTA

4
¡Atención!
Andén número 3 cerrado
por obras

5
Melocotones frescos
– ¡sólo 1.5 euros!

6
¿Estudiante 16–21? Tarifa especial
Autocares Milesa.

7
Sellos, sobres,
papel aquí

8
Clases particulares, inglés
nativo, precios especiales
estudiantes.

A la zapatería
B la estación de RENFE
C la tabacalería/el estanco
D el colegio
E el quiosco

F la pastelería
G la estación de autobuses
H los grandes almacenes
I la frutería

Q Mentally walk along your nearest High Street. Can you make a list of the shops and facilities in Spanish?

B Buying tickets

Learn **key verbs of movement**: <u>llegar</u> (to arrive), <u>salir</u> (to depart/leave), <u>cambiar</u> (to change).

1 In role-play tasks, you need to be able to ask and give information about types of tickets, arrivals and departures.

2 Prepare by revising possible types of tickets.

<u>¿Cómo se dicen en español?</u> How do you ask these in Spanish?

a single ticket to Madrid
a non-smoking ticket
a first-class ticket
a return ticket to Calahorra
two single tickets to Sevilla
a book of ten tickets for the bus

Remember
You do not have to put in the words for 'say', 'ask', 'explain'.

3 The role-play situations in the exam could be informal (you and a friend) or more formal, as here. Work out what you need to say, using the prompt in brackets.

<u>Completa el diálogo.</u> Complete the dialogue.

Empleado/a:	Buenos días, ¿en qué puedo servirle?
Tú:	*(Say you'd like a return ticket to Toledo, please.)*
Empleado/a:	Muy bien. Treinta euros, por favor.
Tú:	*(Ask when the train arrives in Toledo.)*
Empleado/a:	A las doce treinta.
Tú:	*(Ask what platform it goes from.)*
Empleado/a:	Número cinco.
Tú:	*(Ask if you have to change.)*
Empleado/a:	No, es directo.

Q How many other verbs of movement can you remember? Write a list of the Spanish for: to go, to return, to enter, to go up, to go down, to change, to continue.

PRACTICE

Try this exam-type task. In which place or situation (1–7) might you hear each question or request A–F?

<u>Escribe cada letra en la casilla correcta.</u>
Write each letter in the correct box.

A Un café con leche para llevar, por favor.
B ¡Ay, lo siento! ¡He perdido mi billete!
C Un billete de ida y vuelta para Jaén.
D ¿Este es el tren para Cuenca?
E ¿Cuánto cuesta dejar la maleta aquí?
F ¿A qué hora salen los trenes para Valencia mañana?

Think yourself into the situation: imagine yourself in each place. What might you be doing, thinking or wanting to know? Make sure you write down all the letters.

1	En el andén	☐	5 En la consigna	☐
2	En la taquilla	☐	6 En la parada de taxis	☐
3	En la cafetería	☐	7 En el centro de información	☐
4	Hablando con el revisor	☐		

Asking and finding the way

THE BARE BONES

➤ Exchange information about location and facilities.
➤ You need to understand and give directions.

A *Asking where a place is*

KEY FACT

SPEAK

Remember
In questions, use <u>hay</u> followed by <u>un</u> or <u>una</u> except for <u>correos</u>. In the reply, <u>un</u> becomes <u>uno</u>: <u>Hay uno en la plaza.</u> (There is one in the square.)

Q How would you ask where each place in sentences 1–7 is? Use <u>está</u> (singular) or <u>están</u> (plural).

Remember
When <u>de</u> is followed by <u>el</u>, it becomes <u>del</u>.

Q Can you invent similar conversations, beginning with questions 2–7 in Section A?

Learn expressions for asking the way politely.

1 **Stop a passer-by:** Perdone, señor/señora/señorita.

2 **Be polite:** ¿Me puede decir si ...? (*Can you tell me if ...?*)

3 **End courteously:** Muchas gracias (*Many thanks*). De nada (*Don't mention it*).

<u>Usa el mapa para contestar a las preguntas.</u>
Use the map to answer the questions.

Ejemplo: ¿Hay un banco por aquí? – Sí, hay uno en la calle Goya.

1 ¿Hay un estanco por aquí?
2 ¿Hay una cafetería por aquí?
3 ¿Hay una farmacia cerca?
4 ¿Hay servicios por aquí?
5 No veo el mercado. ¿Hay uno?
6 ¿Hay una parada de autobuses por aquí?
7 ¿Hay tiendas turísticas en esta parte de la ciudad?

4 Revise **prepositions of place** ('behind', 'next to', etc.) on pages 26–27.

5 Work out what you need to put in the gaps below, using the map.

Turista: Perdone, señora. ¿Hay un estanco ...(1)... aquí?
Señora: Sí, hay ...(2)... en la Avenida de Cádiz.
Turista: ¿Dónde está exactamente?
Señora: Está ...(3)... del mercado, y ...(4)... la cafetería y las tiendas turísticas.
Turista: Muchas ...(5)... .
Señora: De ...6..., adiós.

B Directions

Remember
Learn useful words like <u>primero</u> (first), <u>luego</u> (then), <u>después</u> (afterwards), <u>finalmente</u> (finally).

Make sure you know your **left** (izquierda) from your **right** (derecha)!

1 Check first that you know your directions!

2 Unscramble the following phrases 1–10. Write the English for each one.

1 la baje calle
2 izquierda a tuerza la
3 izquierda a primera la tome la
4 recto todo siga
5 calle de final al la

6 plaza cruce la
7 a tuerza dercha la
8 la a la tome derecha segunda
9 el siga cruce hasta
10 semáforos los hasta

3 You may have to **read a series of directions**, and **decide where they take you**. Use the map on page 32. Begin at the bottom at (✳).

Lee las instrucciones: ¿adónde llegas?
Escribe el nombre del lugar.

Read the directions. Where do you get to?
Write the name of the place.

1 Siga todo recto. Está al final de la calle Goya, enfrente.

2 Siga hasta el semáforo enfrente del estanco, y luego tuerza a la derecha. Está allí, cerca de la parada de autobús número treinta y dos.

3 Siga todo recto, hasta el cruce. En el semáforo, tuerza a la izquierda. Hay una entrada enfrente de la cafetería.

4 Hay que seguir todo recto, hasta el cruce con el Paseo San Juan, y luego sigue un poco más lejos. Coge la calle a la derecha, y están allí mismo, enfrente.

5 Está a unos cinco minutos andando. Siga todo recto, y coge la calle Goya. Al final, tuerza a la izquierda. La entrada está allí a mano izquierda.

Q Can you work out how to give directions from your home to the nearest shop, to your school, or to the nearest park?

PRACTICE

Answer the questions in Spanish using the map on page 32.

1 Perdone, ¿por dónde se va al Corte Inglés?
2 ¿Para ir al Hotel Buena Vista, por favor?
3 ¿Me puede decir si hay una farmacia por aquí? ¿Cómo se va?
4 ¿Por dónde se va a la cafetería, por favor?

If you realise you've made a mistake in the role-play part of the exam, say <u>Lo siento, me he equivocado,</u> and then try again.

THE BARE BONES

➤ Get the gist of weather forecasts.
➤ Ask for information about an area.
➤ Understand information about a town or region.

A Talking about the weather

KEY FACT

SPEAK

Make sure you know basic weather expressions.

1 You may be asked about the **climate in your area** in the conversation part of the exam, or have to **describe the weather in a role-play**.

2 Practise, using the symbols below.

3 Say what the weather is like in each area.

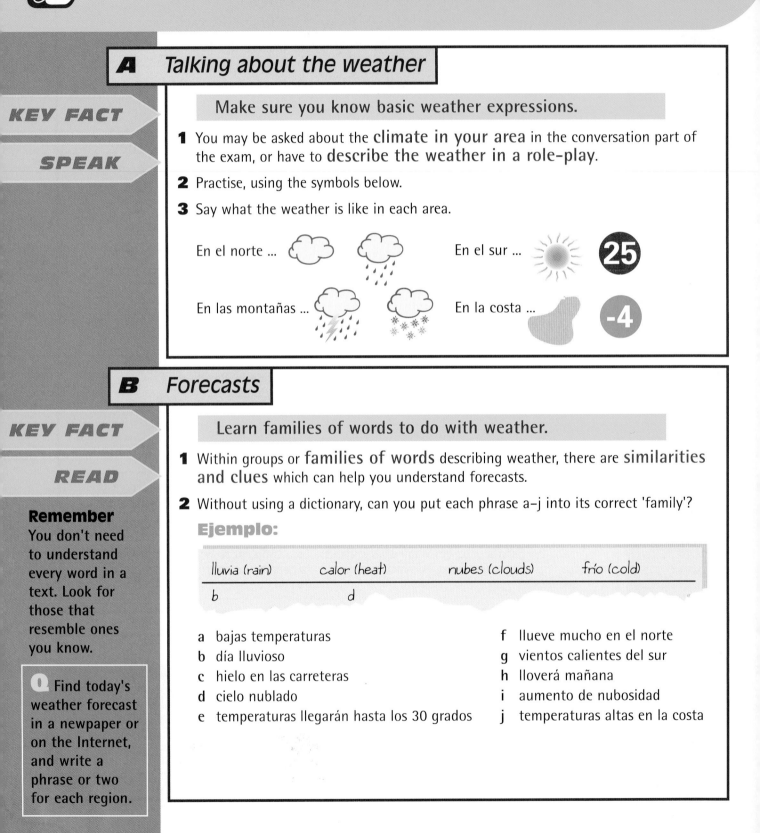

En el norte ...

En las montañas ...

En el sur ... 25

En la costa ... -4

B Forecasts

KEY FACT

READ

Learn families of words to do with weather.

1 Within groups or **families of words** describing weather, there are **similarities and clues** which can help you understand forecasts.

2 Without using a dictionary, can you put each phrase a–j into its correct 'family'?

Ejemplo:

lluvia (rain)	calor (heat)	nubes (clouds)	frío (cold)
b	d		

a bajas temperaturas
b día lluvioso
c hielo en las carreteras
d cielo nublado
e temperaturas llegarán hasta los 30 grados

f llueve mucho en el norte
g vientos calientes del sur
h lloverá mañana
i aumento de nubosidad
j temperaturas altas en la costa

Remember
You don't need to understand every word in a text. Look for those that resemble ones you know.

Q Find today's weather forecast in a newpaper or on the Internet, and write a phrase or two for each region.

C Town and region

With longer pieces of text, you may not need to understand every word.

1 Look at the task first, to see what you are required to do.

2 Try this activity below. Read Mercedes' letter.

Para cada lugar 1–8 escribe la letra del dibujo correcto a–h.
For each place 1–8 write the letter of the correct picture below.

¿Qué tal? Yo bien. Quieres saber algo de mi ciudad, ¿verdad? Vivo en una ciudad pequeña y turística en el sur. Vivo en la parte antigua, cerca del puerto. Es bonita y tiene muchas calles estrechas donde se puede pasear (1). Mi casa está en una plaza pequeña enfrente del ayuntamiento (2). Por la mañana, la zona es muy ruidosa porque hay mucho tráfico (3). De interés histórico, hay la iglesia (4) de San Tomás y bares típicos (5). Hay un castillo y ruinas romanas en las afueras. La ciudad tiene una piscina cerca de la playa con unos jardines preciosos (6), un polideportivo y un centro comercial moderno. Hay una parte al otro lado del río (7), que es industrial y fea. Mi madre trabaja allí en una clínica (8).

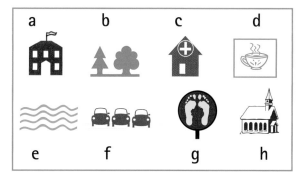

1 g			

3 The Practice activity below gives you an opportunity to try a more challenging task on Mercedes' letter above. Decide whether each sentence is true (**Verdad**), false (**Mentira**) or the text does not say (**No dice**). You may need to search the letter more closely for information, and make some deductions.

Are the following true, false, or the text doesn't say?

1 Mercedes vive en la costa.
2 La parte antigua es fea.
3 Vive en un lugar muy tranquilo.
4 Hay una parte moderna al lado del río.
5 La ciudad tiene monumentos históricos.
6 Hay mucho que hacer para los jóvenes.

Do not assume that the words you see in the sentences 1–6 will necessarily appear in the letter above. Read for meaning!

A Accommodation

Quisiera reservar .../Hice una reserva.	I'd like to reserve .../I made a reservation.
¿Tienes habitaciones libres ... ?	Have you any free rooms ... ?
¿Para cuántas noches/personas?	For how many nights/people?
para esta noche, para (6) noches	for tonight, for (6) nights
desde el (5) hasta el (11) de agosto	from the (5th) to the (11th) of August
¿El desayuno está incluido?	Is breakfast included?
¿A qué nombre?	And your name?/In which name?
¿A qué hora se sirve (la cena)?	What time is (dinner) served?
¿Tiene balcón/vista del mar?	Does it have a balcony/a sea view?
¿Hay sitio para (una tienda familiar)?	Is there room/space for (a family tent)?
¿Dónde se puede (aparcar)?	¿Where can you (park)?
¿Quiere firmar la ficha, por favor?	Can you sign the form, please?

Remember
'Full board' means all meals. 'Half board' means breakfast and one other meal: either lunch or dinner.

un ascensor	the lift	(el) saco de dormir	sleeping-bag
una habitación	a room	... no funciona	... isn't working
doble, individual	double, single	(la) llave, (la) luz	the key, the light
con tres camas	with three beds	no hay (jabón)	there's no (soap)
con ducha/baño	with shower/bath	papel higiénico	toilet paper
pensión completa	full board	(la) pasta de dientes	toothpaste
media pensión	half board	un secador de pelo	hairdryer

B Restaurants

¿Qué quiere tomar (de primero)?	What would you like (for the first course)?
Quisiera, para mi, para mi (amigo/a) ...	I'd like, I'll have, my (friend) will have ...
¿Qué hay para vegetarianos?	What is there for vegetarians?
¿Qué es ... exactamente? ¿Contiene ... ?	What is ... exactly? Does it contain ... ?
¿El servicio está incluido?	Is the service included?
¿Se puede pagar con tarjeta de crédito?	Can I pay with a credit card?
El .../la ... está sucio/a. Falta un/una	The ... is dirty. We're missing a ... .

Remember
El menú is usually a fixed menu, with several choices only, at an all-in-one price. La carta is a fuller menu, with many dishes, each of which is costed individually.

de segundo	for the main course	un vaso, un plato	a glass, a plate
de postre	for dessert	una cuchara	a spoon
para beber	to drink	un cuchillo	a knife
en metálico	in cash	un tenedor	a fork

C Services

No me siento/encuentro bien.	I don't feel well.
¿Qué te/le pasa? Tengo un catarro, tos.	What's the matter? I've got a ... cold, cough.
Me duele el/la ... . Me duelen los/las	My ... hurts. My .... hurt.
¿Desde hace cuánto tiempo?	For how long?
desde ayer; desde hace (dos) días	since yesterday; for the last (two) days
Tome estas pastillas; Ponga esta crema.	Take these tablets; Put on this cream.

Remember
With desde hace, use the present tense: me duele desde hace un mes. (It's been hurting for a month.)

D The preterite tense

The preterite tense explains what happened.
For example: *I went to Spain; I visited the capital; I ate out at night.*

The following are regular.

	-ar (hablar)	-er (comer)	-ir (vivir)
yo	hablé	comí	viví
tú	hablaste	comiste	viviste
él, ella, usted	habló	comió	vivió
nosotros	hablamos	comimos	vivimos
vosotros	hablasteis	comisteis	vivisteis
ellos, ellas, ustedes	hablaron	comieron	vivieron

The following are irregular. Note that **ser** *(to be)* and **ir** *(to go)* are the same.

SER *(TO BE)*	fui, fuiste, fue, fuimos, fuisteis, fueron
IR *(TO GO)*	fui, fuiste, fue, fuimos, fuisteis, fueron
DAR *(TO GIVE)*	dí, diste, dio, dimos, disteis, dieron

Remember
Some regular verbs many need to change their spelling to keep the same sound, e.g. <u>cruzar</u> (to cross) → <u>yo crucé</u> (I crossed); <u>llegar</u> (to arrive) → <u>yo llegué</u> (I arrived)

E The pretérito grave

The following verbs have a change to their stem, and different endings.
(The stem is the part which is left when you remove the **-ar, -er, -ir**).

INFINITIVE		STEM	INFINITIVE		STEM
to walk	andar	anduv-	to put, lay, set	poner	pus-
to say	decir	dij-	to want to	querer	quis-
to be	estar	estuv-	to know	saber	sup-
to do, make	hacer	hic-	to have	tener	tuv-
to be able to	poder	pud-	to come	venir	vin-

Add these endings to the stems above:

yo	-e	nosotros	-imos
tú	-iste	vosotros	-isteis
él, ella, usted	-o	ellos, ellas, ustedes	-ieron

Estuve en el centro todo el día.	I was in the centre all day.
Hicimos mucho turísmo.	We did a lot of sightseeing.

Remember
<u>Hacer</u> has a spelling change to keep the same sound: <u>yo hice</u>, but <u>él, ella, usted hizo</u>.

F Time phrases

You will find the following time phrases useful:

ayer, anteayer	*yesterday, the day before yesterday*
anoche, hace dos días	*last night, two days ago*
el año pasado, la semana pasada	*last year, last week*

Accommodation

THE BARE BONES
➤ Ask for and understand information about accommodation.
➤ Write a letter to book somewhere to stay.

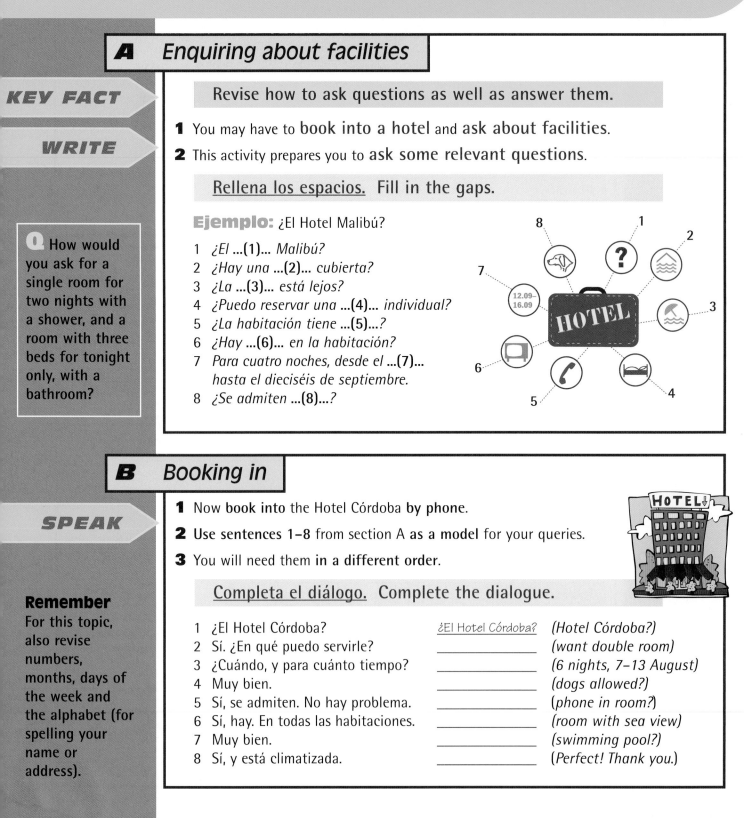

KEY FACT

WRITE

A Enquiring about facilities

Revise how to ask questions as well as answer them.

1 You may have to book into a hotel and ask about facilities.

2 This activity prepares you to ask some relevant questions.

Rellena los espacios. Fill in the gaps.

Ejemplo: ¿El Hotel Malibú?

1 ¿El ...(1)... Malibú?
2 ¿Hay una ...(2)... cubierta?
3 ¿La ...(3)... está lejos?
4 ¿Puedo reservar una ...(4)... individual?
5 ¿La habitación tiene ...(5)...?
6 ¿Hay ...(6)... en la habitación?
7 Para cuatro noches, desde el ...(7)... hasta el dieciséis de septiembre.
8 ¿Se admiten ...(8)...?

Q How would you ask for a single room for two nights with a shower, and a room with three beds for tonight only, with a bathroom?

B Booking in

SPEAK

1 Now book into the Hotel Córdoba by phone.

2 Use sentences 1–8 from section A as a model for your queries.

3 You will need them in a different order.

Completa el diálogo. Complete the dialogue.

1 ¿El Hotel Córdoba? — ¿El Hotel Córdoba? (Hotel Córdoba?)
2 Sí. ¿En qué puedo servirle? — _____ (want double room)
3 ¿Cuándo, y para cuánto tiempo? — _____ (6 nights, 7–13 August)
4 Muy bien. — _____ (dogs allowed?)
5 Sí, se admiten. No hay problema. — _____ (phone in room?)
6 Sí, hay. En todas las habitaciones. — _____ (room with sea view)
7 Muy bien. — _____ (swimming pool?)
8 Sí, y está climatizada. — _____ (Perfect! Thank you.)

Remember
For this topic, also revise numbers, months, days of the week and the alphabet (for spelling your name or address).

C Campsites

Read for meaning and use your knowledge of grammar.

1 The following exam-type task asks you to complete the letter by **choosing the correct word for each gap** from the list below it.

2 There will be **more words than gaps**, and **some of them may be very similar.**

3 Use the following hints to help:

- After **quiero, quisiera, puedo,** Spanish often needs a verb in the infinitive form.
- After **del**, you will need a masculine singular noun.
- After a number, you may need a plural noun.
- After a noun, you may need an adjective.

Escribe la letra correcta en cada casilla.
Write the correct letter in each box.

Remember
Try and understand the meaning of the sentences, e.g. you will not want to put word D in the final box!

Q How would you ask if there's room for a caravan, and three young people?

A visitar
B pequeñas
C playa
D aseos
E chicos
F bicicletas
G reserva
H saber
I personas
J pueblo
K habitación
L espacio

Muy señor mío,

Quisiera ☐ el sur de España durante el mes de mayo. Le ruego me reserve ☐ en el camping para cinco noches entre el dos y el siete de mayo. Somos cinco ☐ en total: dos adultos, un joven de dieciséis años, y dos niños de ocho años y diez años. Tenemos un coche, una tienda familiar y dos tiendas ☐.

Quiero ☐ también si el camping tiene un supermercado, y a qué distancia del ☐ está. ¿Se puede alquilar ☐?

Le saluda atentamente,

Francisco Aguilar Montero.

PRACTICE

Write a letter in Spanish to a campsite with the following information. Use the letter above as a model.

- north of Spain
- 7 nights
- 22–29 July
- 3 adults
- 3 children (6, 9, 11)
- two cars

- two family tents
- two small tents
- Is there a pool?
- How far to the beach?
- Hire boats?

Check your spelling! If you make an error in a key word which means you have written a different Spanish word, you will lose marks. Take care here with plaza/playa and junio/julio.

Holiday activities

THE BARE BONES
➤ Understand information in restaurants and cafés
➤ Order food and drink
➤ Exchange information and opinions about holidays

A On holiday

KEY FACT

READ

Watch out for negatives: they can change the meaning.

1 This next activity **tests your ability** to understand **negatives** and **opposites**.

2 Revise **no ... nada** *(nothing)*, **no ... nunca** *(never)*, **no ... nadie** *(no-one)*.
Take particular care with sentences 3, 5 and 7.

Remember
Negatives like <u>nunca</u>, <u>nadie</u>, <u>nada</u> can also come at the start of a sentence, in which case they lose the <u>no</u>.

Elige la palabra correcta para cada frase.
Choose the correct word for each sentence.

1 Teresa está de vacaciones con sus _____ .

2 El hotel es _____ .

3 La playa no está _____ .

4 La comida es _____ .

5 En general, no hace _____ tiempo.

6 No llueve _____ .

7 Como deporte, le gusta hacer _____ .

> ¡Hola! ¿Qué tal? Estoy aquí de vacaciones con Mamá y Papá. El hotel es precioso y grande, y está cerca de la playa. Me gusta la comida – es muy rica. A veces hace viento, pero en general hace calor. Y nada de lluvia – ¡qué bien! Juego al voleibol en la playa y nado en la piscina. A veces, voy de compras en el pueblo que es muy antiguo. El sábado, voy a ir de excursión a la montaña.
>
> Teresa.

hermanos   buena   equitación   bonito   mucho   padres
cerca   mal   nunca   lejos   cómodo   natación

B Using different tenses

WRITE

1 In the writing exam, you may be given prompts in English. Try this activity in preparation. Reply to Teresa and tell her:

1 Where you are spending your holidays *(in Scotland)*.

2 What the town is like *(pretty, touristy)*.

3 What you are doing *(visiting castles, walking on beach/coast)*.

4 What the weather is like *(quite warm, rains sometimes)*.

5 What you did yesterday *(hired a bike)*.

6 What you are going to do at the weekend *(go on a boat trip)*.

Remember
If you are aiming for higher grades, make sure you use past, present and future tenses.

C Restaurants

Remember
If the instruction asks you to tick four boxes, do tick four even if you're not sure – there aren't any marks for leaving a blank space.

Make sure you know a range of common dishes and foods.

1 You read the following menu in a restaurant window.

¿Qué se puede comer? Escribe ✔ en 4 casillas .
What can you eat? Put a ✔ in 4 boxes.

Menú del día

Gazpacho andaluz
Ensaladilla rusa
Zumos

＊＊＊

Hamburguesas con queso
Tortilla española
Filete de ternera

＊＊＊

Piña en almibar
Flan
Tarta de limón con nata

1 pescado ☐
2 carne ☐
3 huevos ☐
4 legumbres ☐
5 helados ☐
6 fruta ☐
7 pasteles ☐

2 Revise phrases for ordering food and drink.

Explica lo que quieres comer y beber.
Explain what you want to eat and drink.

Camarero/a:	Buenas tardes, señores. ¿Qué va a tomar?	
Tú:	De primero, quiero …	○○○○○◯ tomato salad
Camarero/a:	¿Y de segundo?	
Tú:	Me gustaría probar …	○○○○○◯ Spanish omelette and chips
Camarero/a:	¿Y de postre?	
Tú:	Para mí …	○○○○○◯ strawberry ice-cream
Camarero/a:	¿Y para beber?	
Tú:	Quisiera …	○○○○◯ fizzy mineral water

Q How would you say: 'Is there anything for vegetarians?' 'What do you recommend?' 'What is … exactly?' 'Service included?'

PRACTICE

You have just finished an exchange visit to Spain.

Write an article in Spanish (about 120–150 words) for their regional magazine.

Make sure you use tenses in the past, future and present tenses. Add descriptive adjectives, and opinions to improve marks for quality of language.

- con quién fuiste y cómo
- cuánto tiempo te quedaste
- lo que visitaste
- algún excursión que hiciste
- tu opinión de tu estancia en España
- lo que quieres hacer el año próximo

➤ Explain why you're not feeling well.
➤ Talk about a loss or theft.

A Parts of the body

KEY FACT

WRITE

Remember
With el/la, use me duele, e.g. 'Me duele la cabeza.' With los/las, use me duelen, e.g. 'Me duelen los pies.'

Q How would you say that each of the parts of the body 1–14 is hurting?

Revise the Spanish for the parts of the body.

1 If you're ill, you'll need to be able to **explain what is wrong** with you.

2 How many **parts of the body** do you know?

Completa cada palabra con las letras que faltan.
Complete each word with the letters which are missing.

1 la cab- - - (*head*)
2 la nar- - (*nose*)
3 los oíd- - (*ears*)
4 la boc- (*mouth*)
5 la mu- - - (*tooth*)
6 la garg- - - - (*throat*)
7 los oj- - (*eyes*)

8 la espal- - (*back*)
9 el bra- - (*arm*)
10 la ma- - (*hand*)
11 el de- - (*finger*)
12 el estóm- - - (*stomach*)
13 la pie- - - (*leg*)
14 el pi- (*foot*)

B Explaining what's the matter

SPEAK

Remember
Further back in time than yesterday needs desde hace, e.g. no me siento bien desde hace dos días. (I haven't been feeling well for two days.)

Q Can you explain you have hay fever (fiebre del heno), and sunstroke (insolación).

1 You may have to take part in a role-play where **you are feeling ill**.

Sustituye las expresiones subrayadas por otras apropiadas. Replace the underlined expressions by other appropriate ones.

+ ¿Qué tal?
* No me encuentro bien.
+ ¿Qué te pasa?
* Me duele la garganta.
+ ¿Desde hace cuánto tiempo no te sientes bien?
* Desde ayer.
+ ¿Tienes otros síntomas?
* Tengo catarro también.
+ Vamos a ver ...

la cabeza
no me siento bien
desde hace dos días
no estoy muy bien
el estómago
náuseas
fiebre
desde anoche

C Lost property

You may not need to understand every word.

1 Explaining you've lost an item usually involves **a range of tenses**: where you lost it, what it was like, when you will be returning home.

2 Though the **language may be more complex**, the **task might be quite simple**.

3 Study carefully what you have to do. The activity below simply asks you to tick the pictures which reflect what happened.

Escribe ✓ en cada casilla apropiada.
Put a ✓ in each appropriate box.

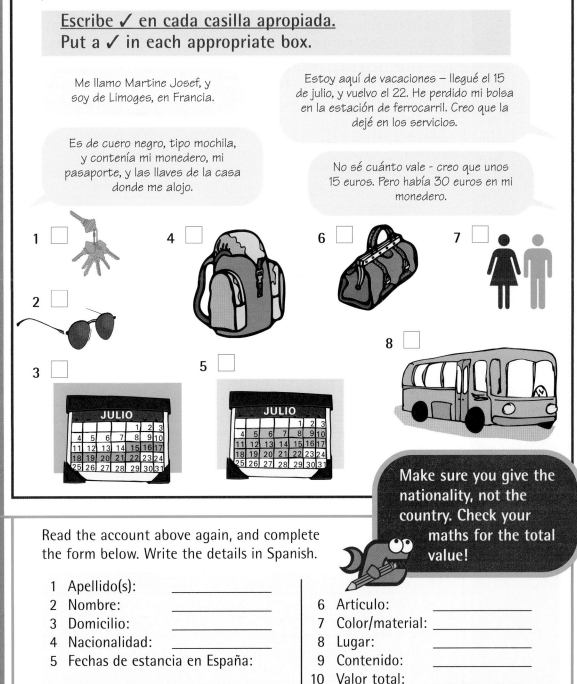

Me llamo Martine Josef, y soy de Limoges, en Francia.

Estoy aquí de vacaciones – llegué el 15 de julio, y vuelvo el 22. He perdido mi bolsa en la estación de ferrocarril. Creo que la dejé en los servicios.

Es de cuero negro, tipo mochila, y contenía mi monedero, mi pasaporte, y las llaves de la casa donde me alojo.

No sé cuánto vale - creo que unos 15 euros. Pero había 30 euros en mi monedero.

Read the account above again, and complete the form below. Write the details in Spanish.

Make sure you give the nationality, not the country. Check your maths for the total value!

1 Apellido(s): _____
2 Nombre: _____
3 Domicilio: _____
4 Nacionalidad: _____
5 Fechas de estancia en España:
   _____

6 Artículo: _____
7 Color/material: _____
8 Lugar: _____
9 Contenido: _____
10 Valor total: _____

Vocabulary

A Household chores

¿Tienes que ayudar en casa?	Do you have to help at home?
¿Qué tienes que hacer?	What do you have to do?
Tengo que (hacer mi cama).	I have to (make my bed).
¿Qué tiene que hacer tu (hermano)?	What does your (brother) have to do?
Tiene que (lavar/fregar los platos).	S/he has to (wash the dishes).
¿Hay algún quehacer que no te guste?	Is there a chore which you don't like?
Odio/detesto (poner la mesa)	I hate (setting the table)
... porque es aburrido/pesado.	... because it's boring.

barrer el suelo	to sweep the floor	quitar el polvo	to dust
cortar la hierba	to cut the grass	quitar la mesa	to clear the table
lavar el coche	to wash the car	poner la mesa	to set/lay the table
lavar la ropa	to wash the clothes	recoger el salón	to tidy the lounge
limpiar por todo	to clean everywhere	regar las plantas	to water the plants
pasar la aspiradora	to vacuum-clean	sacar la basura	the take out the rubbish
planchar	to iron	sacar al perro	to take the dog out

B Healthy living

¿Qué haces para estar sano/a, en forma?	What do you do to be healthy, fit?
¿Qué hay que hacer para ...	What do you have to do in order to ...
llevar una vida sana?	lead a healthy life?
¿Qué vas a hacer tú?	What are you going to do?
Hago ejercicio, duermo/como bien.	I take exercise, I sleep/eat well.
Hay que (beber menos alcohol).	You have to (drink less alcohol).
Se debe (dormir siete horas al día).	You ought (to sleep for seven hours a day).
Hace falta (respetar el cuerpo).	It's necessary to (respect one's body).

acostarse	to go to bed	seguir	to follow
más temprano	earlier	una dieta sana	a healthy diet
evitar el estrés	to avoid stress	es dañino ...	it's harmful ...
no fumar	not to smoke	al corazón	to the heart
no tomar drogas / no drogarse	not to take drugs	al pecho	to the chest
no drogarse		a los pulmones	to the lungs
no emborracharse	not to get drunk	es peligroso	it's dangerous
relajarse	to relax	es bueno/malo	it's good/bad
estar en regimen	to be on a diet	para la salud	for one's health

la comida nutritiva	nourishing food	menos grasa	less fat
comidas preparadas	ready-made meals	menos sal	less salt
la alimentación sana	healthy food	más fruta	more fruit
la comida basura	junk food	más verduras	more vegetables
un alimento	a foodstuff, food	menos estimulantes	fewer stimulants
comer, tomar	to eat, take/have	más vitaminas	more vitamins

C Leisure

Remember
f you're not
sure of your size,
say <u>No estoy
seguro/a</u>. <u>Creo
que es</u> ... ('I'm
not sure. I think
t's ...')

¿Qué ponen en la tele/el cine?	What's on TV/at the cinema?
Ponen una película de acción/de terror.	There's an action/horror film on.
una película de ciencia-ficción.	A science-fiction film.
una película de aventura, una telenovela	An adventure film, a soap-opera.
una película romántica/policíaca	A romantic/detective film.
¿Cuánto cuestan las entradas?	How much are the tickets?
¿Dónde están los asientos? Arriba/abajo.	Where are the seats? Upstairs/downstairs.
¿A qué hora empieza/termina (la sesión)?	What time does the (showing) start/finish?

un baile	a dance	un documental	a documentary
una cartelera	an entertainment guide	una función	a show
una comedia	a comedy	un partido	a match
un concierto	a concert	la publicidad	advertising
un concurso	a quiz-show, contest	las noticias	the news (bulletin)
una corrida	a bull fight	el telediario	the news (information)
los toros	the bulls	la taquilla	the box-office
dibujos animados	cartoons	un anuncio	an announcement/ advertisement

D Shopping

Remember
Having
problems? Use
<u>es demasiado</u> ...
(it's too ...)
<u>corto/a</u> (short),
<u>largo/a</u> (long),
<u>estrecho/a</u>
(narrow, tight),
<u>holgado/a</u>
(baggy), <u>caro/a</u>
(expensive).

¿Dónde puedo comprar ...? Busco ...	Where can I buy ... ? I'm looking for ...
¿Tiene ... ? ¿Hay ... ? ¿Se vende ... ?	Do you have ... ? Are there ... ? Do you sell ... ?
Quisiera ... . ¿Me pone/da ... por favor?	I'd like ... . Can you give me ... please?
¿Es todo? Sí, es todo.	Is that everything? Yes, that's the lot.
¿Algo más? No, nada más, gracias.	Anything else? No, nothing else, thanks.
¿Tiene cambio? No tengo cambio.	Have you got any change? I don't have change.
Sólo tengo un billete de (50) euros.	I've only got a (50) euro note.
¿Se puede pagar con un cheque?	Can you pay by cheque?
con tarjeta de crédito, en metálico/efectivo	by credit card, in cash
¿Qué tamaño? Grande, pequeño, mediano	What size? Big, small, medium
¿Qué talla usa? La (40). (clothes)	What size do you take? Size (40).
¿Qué número calza? El (38). (shoes)	What size shoe do you take? Size (38).

un abrigo	a coat	un pantalón	a pair of trousers
un bañador	a swimming costume	un pantalón corto	a pair of shorts
una blusa/una camisa	a blouse/a shirt	la ropa	clothes
una camiseta	a T-shirt	un sombrero	a hat
un chandal	a track suit	un gorro	a cap
un cinturón	a belt	las medias/los calecetines	stockings/socks
una corbata	a tie	los guantes	gloves
una falda	a skirt	los vaqueros	jeans
un impermeable	a raincoat	zapatos, zapatillas	shoes, slippers
un jersey	a jersey	zapatillas deportivas	trainers

una barra de ...	a loaf of ...	una caja de ...	a box of ...
una bolsa de ...	a bag of ...	un tubo de ...	a tube of ...
una botella de ...	a bottle of ...	un paquete de ...	a packet of ...
un bote de ...	a jar of ...	un kilo/litro de ...	a kilo/litre of ...

A Direct object pronouns

Direct object pronouns in English are: *me, you, him, her, it, us, them*. In Spanish they are:

SINGULAR		PLURAL	
me	*me*	nos	*us*
te	*you (informal)*	os	*you (informal)*
le, lo, la	*it, him; it, her*	los (*m*), las (*f*)	*them (objects)*
le (*m*), la (*f*)	*you (formal)*	les (*m*), las (*f*)	*them (people) you (formal)*

Note that for OBJECTS you need to use **lo, la, los** and **las**. For PEOPLE, use **le, la, les, las**.

¿Qué? No te oigo bien.	*What? I can't hear you clearly.*
¿El bañador? Sí, lo compro.	*The swimming costume? Yes, I'm buying it.*
La falda … . No la quiero.	*The skirt … . I don't want it.*
¿Los calcetines? Sí, los llevo.	*The socks? Yes, I'll take them.*
¿Juan? No le veo.	*Juan? I don't see him.*

1 Put the following into Spanish, using the prompt in brackets.

Ejemplo: a Quiero comprar este jersey.

a Quiero comprar_____ jersey. *(this)*

b ¿Cuánto cuesta_____ camisa? *(that)*

c ¿Ves_____ pantalón? *(that over there)*

d ¿La corbata roja? Si, *(that one)*.

e ¿Le gustan los sombreros? *(those ones)*.

f Busco sandalias *(those ones, over there)*.

B Demonstrative adjectives and pronouns

Use demonstrative adjectives for *this …, that …, those …*:

	(*ms*)	(*fs*)		(*mpl*)	(*fpl*)
this	este	esta	*these*	estos	estas
that	ese	esa	*those*	esos	esas
that (over there)	aquel	aquella	*those (over there)*	aquellos	aquellas

No me gusta esta chaqueta.	*I don't like this jacket.*
Ese chandal es caro.	*That track-suit is expensive.*
Aquel cinturón es más barato.	*That belt over there is cheaper.*
Aquellos vaqueros son bonitos.	*Those jeans over there are nice.*

Demonstrative pronouns (*this one, that one, those ones*) are the same as the demonstrative adjectives above, but carry an accent on the first 'e':

¿Un abrigo? – ¿Te gusta éste?	*A coat? – Do you like this one?*
Quiero una camiseta. – ¿Cuánto es ésa?	*I want a T-shirt. – How much is that one?*

C Verbs of obligation

There are several ways of expressing the idea of *having* to do something.
Each of them are followed by the infinitive:

Tener que ... *(have to, must)*	Deber ... *(ought to, should)*	Hay que ... *(one has to)*

Tengo que hacerlo ahora.	*I have to do it now. (No choice!)*
Debo hacerlo ahora.	*I ought to do it now. (But I might decide not to.)*
Hay que trabajar mucho.	*One has to work hard. (Idea of necessity.)*

2 Change these sentences using the verb in brackets, and write the English meaning:

Ejemplo: Debo recoger mi dormitorio. *I ought to tidy my room.*

a Tengo que hacer mi cama. (deber)
b Todos debemos ayudar en casa. (tener que)
c Debes aprender el vocabulario, si quieres aprobar el examen. (hay que)
d Los jóvenes tienen que hacer más ejercicio físico. (deber)
e Felipe, hay que coger las entradas para el cine. (tener que)
f Anita y Paco, tenéis que recoger el salón. (hay que)

D Se

Using **se** with the third person of the verb is equivalent in English to *one ..., they ..., people ...,
you/we ...* . It indicates what generally happens or is done:

En España, se bebe más café.	*In Spain, they drink more coffee.*
Se come menos grasa animal.	*People eat less animal fat.*
Se toma más ejercicio en verano.	*One does more exercise in summer.*
Aquí se habla inglés.	*English is spoken here.*

When the item following the verb is plural, you need the third person plural of the verb
(**ellos/ellas/ustedes**):

¿Se venden sombreros de paja?	*Do you sell straw hats here?*
Se comen más patatas en Gran Bretaña.	*They/we eat more potatoes in Great Britain.*
Se hablan catalán y castellano en Cataluña.	*Catalan and Spanish are spoken in Cataluña.*

3 Put the verbs in brackets into the correct form, using **se**.

Ejemplo: En España, se bebe más café que té ...

En España, (beber) más café que té, y (comer) más verduras y fruta que aquí en Gran Bretaña.
(Tomar) menos grasa animal también. Pero (fumar) más cigarrillos en los lugares públicos.
No (tomar) tantos dulces, aunque el turrón que (fabricar) cerca de Alicante es muy popular
en Navidad.

Chores and healthy living

THE BARE BONES

➤ Learn to say which chores you and other people do.
➤ Say what you do to stay healthy.

A Staying healthy

READ

1 You may get **several texts** written by different people to read.

2 First read the instructions below. Then **look for words you associate with each topic.**

3 Tick the box as soon as you meet a topic in one text: you don't need to look for it in all of them.

4 **Take care with negatives:** someone saying they don't smoke still means the theme is mentioned!

Remember
Both <u>pero</u> and <u>sino</u> mean 'but'. Use <u>sino</u> after a negative: <u>no como dos tabletas de chocolate, sino tres</u>. (I don't eat two bars of chocolate, but three.)

> ¿Se habla de cada tema A–H? Escribe ✔ en las casillas correctas.
> Is each topic A–H mentioned? Put a ✔ in the correct boxes.

A la comida ☐   C el beber ☐   E no estar bien ☐   G los quehaceres ☐

B el ejercicio físico ☐   D el estrés ☐   F el fumar ☐   H las drogas ☐

Q Use the verbs in the texts to write a few lines about your own healthy (or unhealthy!) habits.

Soy muy deportista. Hago footing dos veces a la semana, y voy a la piscina el sábado. No bebo alcohol – es malo para la salud. Muchos de mis amigos fuman pero yo no. Sigo un régimen sano. Siempre desayuno, almuerzo en la cantina de la fábrica y por la tarde, ceno fruta y yogur.

Joaquín

Yo soy adicto al chocolate (dos tabletas cada día), y a los cigarillos – no fumo dos o tres, sino ocho o diez cada día. No tomo nunca ejercicio. Pero no tomo drogas. Todos los días, me digo que voy a cambiar, que voy a hacer ejercicio y comer bien – pero no lo hago.

Paco

Me levanto temprano todos los días para hacer yoga, y voy a mi trabajo andando. Nunca uso el coche entre semana. El fin de semana, me gusta salir de la ciudad a la montaña e ir de paseo. Tomo un poco de vino con la cena cada noche, pero aparte de eso, no bebo.

Alicia

B Reading for detail

1 Now read the same texts again **for detail.**

2 Take care with **expressions of degree:** words like **bastante** (*quite a lot*), **bien** (*well*), **muy** (*very*).

3 Look out for **time phrases** like **todos los días** (*every day*), **nunca** (*never*), **entre semana** (*during the week*).

B

4 <u>Para cada frase a–f, escribe el nombre de la persona apropiada.</u>
For each sentence a–f, write the name of the appropriate person.

a Le gusta ir a pie. _____

b Fuma bastante. _____

c Toma ejercicio físico todos los días. _____

d Come bien. _____

e No bebe nunca. _____

f Es muy perezoso/a. _____

C Chores

KEY FACT

After the key phrases <u>tengo que</u>, <u>ayudo a</u> and <u>suelo</u>, use the infinitive form of the verb.

WRITE

1 Use the beginnings of sentences below to describe what **chores you do**, and **others in your family do**.

Remember
<u>Suelo ...</u>, followed by the infinitive, means 'to ... usually' (do something): e.g. <u>Suelo lavar los platos.</u> (I usually wash the dishes.)

Explaining what you do	Explaining what other people do
Tengo que ...... *I have to ......* Ayudo a ...... *I help to ......* Suelo ...... *I usually ......*	Mi (padre) tiene que ...... *My (father) has to ......* Mi (hermano) ayuda a ...... *My (brother) helps to ....*

<u>Completa cada frase en español.</u>
Complete each sentence in Spanish.

1 Todos los días, tengo que _____ . *(tidy my room)*

2 Mi hermana tiene que _____ o lavar los platos. *(set the table)*

3 El fin de semana, tengo que ayudar a _____ por toda la casa. *(vacuum-clean)*

4 Mi padre tiene que _____ entresemana. *(prepare the evening meal)*

5 Mi madrastra suele _____ después de trabajar. *(do the shopping)*

6 ¿Y tú? ¿Qué tienes que hace para _____ en casa? *(to help)*

Q Can you write a sentence for each member of your family, explaining which chores each person does, and when.

PRACTICE

Prepare your replies in Spanish to the following questions which you might be asked in the conversation part of the exam.

¿Qué tienes que hacer para ayudar en casa?
¿Tienes que ayudar entre semana?
¿Qué tienen que hacer tus padres?
¿Hay algún quehacer que no te guste? ¿Por qué?
¿Te parece bien que tienes que ayudar en casa? ¿Por qué?

Make sure to give your opinion wherever you can. You might find these adjectives useful: <u>aburrido/pesado</u> (boring), <u>necesario</u> (necessary), <u>útil</u> (useful), <u>una pérdida de tiempo</u> (a waste of time).

Leisure

THE BARE BONES
➤ Revise making arrangements to meet.
➤ Give your opinion on TV programmes and films.

A Invitations

Learn time phrases with el, por, de.

1 When arranging to go out, you may need to mention:

- a day (e.g. on Friday)
- a specific time (e.g. at 11a.m)
- a general time of day (e.g. the morning)

Day of the week: use **el**	¿Quieres salir el viernes? *Do you want to go out on Friday?*
General time of day: use **por**	Te llamo por la tarde, ¿vale? *I'll ring you in the afternoon, OK?*
Specific time of day: use **de**	¿Nos vemos a las diez de la noche? *Shall we meet at 10p.m?*

Remember
Other useful time phrases are: <u>esta mañana</u> (this morning), <u>esta tarde</u> (this afternoon/ evening) and <u>esta noche</u> (tonight).

2 ### Rellena cada espacio con el, por o de.
Fill each gap with el, por or de.

Javi:	¡Oiga, Marifé! Soy Javi. ¿Quieres ir al cine conmigo ...(1)... viernes?
Marifé:	Lo siento. Tengo que ir al centro con Alicia a las dos ...(2)... la tarde.
Javi:	Vamos todos a la discoteca el sábado ...(3)... la noche – ¿quieres venir?
Marifé:	Lo siento. Tengo que cuidar a mi hermano. ¿Estás libre ...(4)... domingo?
Javi:	...(5)... la tarde solamente.
Marifé:	No sé. Voy a hablar con mamá. Te llamo mañana ...(6)... la mañana, ¿vale?

3 ### Inventa otra conversación. Utiliza estos detalles.
Invent another conversation. Use these details.

- Javi invites Marifé to the bowling alley. She can't go, as she's going to the swimming pool.
- Javi suggests the ice-rink but Marifé has to look after her sister.
- Javi is only free on Sunday night, so Marifé promises to ring him in the afternoon.

Q How many places of entertainment can you name in Spanish? E.g. <u>el cine</u> ...

B TV and film

READ

1 You need to be able to **give your own view**, both **positive** and **negative**.

2 Try to **add phrases** which indicate **what you think**: creo que/pienso que (*I think that*), **en mi opinión** (*in my opinion*).

> ¿Cuál es la opinión de cada persona? Escribe P (positiva), N (negativa) o P+N (positiva y negativa).
>
> What is the opinion of each person? Write P (positive), N (negative), or P+N (positive and negative).

Ejemplo: Miguel – P

Alicia		Pablo	
Santiago		Teresa	
Belén		Eduardo	

Los programas deportivos no me interesan mucho. **Eduardo**

Creo que las comedias son buenas. Me gusta mucho el humor. Santiago

Creo que las películas románticas son emocionantes. Vi 'Chocolate' la semana pasada, y me gustó mucho el ambiente. **Miguel**

En mi opinión, las películas de ciencia-ficción son estupendas. Vi la serie 'Stars Wars' hace poco, y lo mejor era los efectos especiales. **Belén**

Los westerns son malos. A veces el paisaje es bonito, pero los protagonistas no son interesantes. Pablo

Pienso que las películas de aventuras son emocionantes, pero lo peor es la violencia. **Teresa**

¿Los dibujos animados? En general son divertidos, pero a veces son tontos. Alicia

Q Make a list of the adjectives in the comments. Which others do you know that might be useful here?

Adjectives need to agree with the noun they describe: <u>los westerns son aburridos, las comedias son divertidas.</u>

PRACTICE

Write a short paragraph in Spanish about TV programmes or films you like or dislike, and say why. Include a brief account of a film you've seen recently. Use the comments above, and the following phrases, to help.

me gustan/encantan	I like/love
no me gustan/odio	I hate
Vi una película de acción que se llama	I saw an action film called ... .
Fui al cine (el sábado pasado).	I went to the cinema (last Saturday).
Fue/era muy (emocionante).	It was very (exciting).
lo mejor/peor fue ...	the best/worst was ...

Shopping

THE BARE BONES
➤ Buy food items, presents and items of clothing.
➤ Talk or write about your shopping preferences.

A Clothes

KEY FACT

READ

Learn verb endings. They give you the information about who is speaking.

1 Look carefully in a text at what the writer is saying about him/herself: **yo ...** *(I ...)*, **me gusta** *(I like)*.

2 Don't be misled by how the verb is describing what others are doing: **mis amigos ...** *(my friends)*, **otras personas ...** *(other people)*.

Remember
también means 'also'. Tampoco (neither) is used after a negative.

Q Can you name two things in Spanish you might wear on your head, something which goes round your neck, two garments for covering the top half of your body, two for your lower half, and three you might wear on your feet?

Lee lo que escribe Amalia, y elige la frase correcta a, b, o c.
Read what Amalia says and choose the correct phrase a, b, or c.

1 En cuanto a ropa, Amalia ...
   a) gasta mucho dinero
   b) gasta poco
   c) no gasta nada

2 Al instituto, le gusta llevar ...
   a) la ropa tipo sport
   b) ir a la moda
   c) la ropa cómoda

3 No le gustan las prendas de ...
   a) algodón
   b) cuero
   c) nilón

4 Prefiere llevar los colores ...
   a) oscuros
   b) claros
   c) vivos

5 Si va a una fiesta, prefiere la ropa ...
   a) original
   b) elegante
   c) de marca

6 Compra en ...
   a) los grandes almacenes
   b) las tiendas pequeñas
   c) el mercado

I A mí, no me interesa mucho la moda. Mis padres me dan dinero para comprar ropa, pero no gasto mucho.

2 Cuando voy al colegio, llevo vaqueros y un jersey o una camisa. Algunos de mis amigos siempre van a la moda, o llevan ropa tipo sport (chandal, con zapatillas deportivas) pero yo no.

3 Algunos de mi clase llevan las telas sintéticas, como el nilón o el poliéster, pero yo prefiero las naturales, como el lino, el algodón o el cuero.

4 Soy morena, y por eso me van bien los colores alegres, como el rojo y el amarillo – no me gustan los colores tristes como el negro o el marrón, ni los aburridos como el azul claro o el color rosa.

5 No suelo llevar prendas de marca y no soy muy original tampoco. Para salir con amigos o ir a una fiesta, me gusta ponerme una falda larga y una chaqueta.

6 Cuando voy de compras, me gusta mirar los escaparates de los grandes almacenes, o ver lo que hay en el mercado, pero normalmente encuentro lo que busco en los boutiques.

B Food shopping

WRITE

1 For supermarket shopping, you will need to know a **wide range of things to eat and drink.**

2 Make sure you learn the Spanish for **different types of containers.**

Remember
If you only want half a litre or half a kilo, use <u>medio litro/medio kilo</u>. <u>Un cuarto de kilo</u> (a quarter of a kilo) is the same as <u>doscientos cincuenta gramos</u> (250 grams).

<u>Completa la lista de compras con alimentos o bebidas apropiados.</u> Complete the shopping list with appropriate items of food or drink.

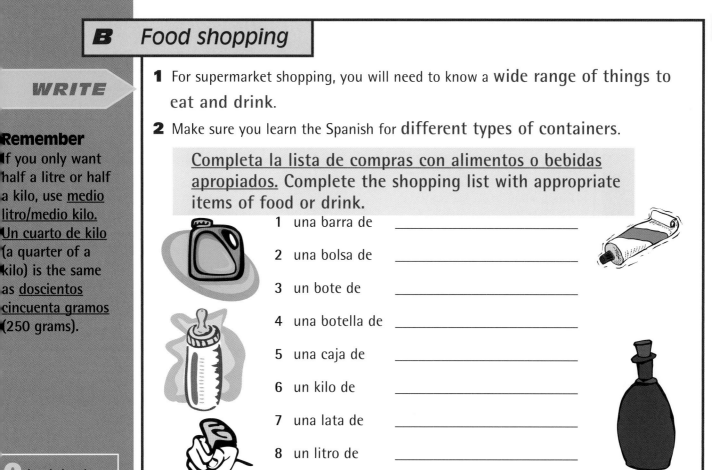

1 una barra de _____

2 una bolsa de _____

3 un bote de _____

4 una botella de _____

5 una caja de _____

6 un kilo de _____

7 una lata de _____

8 un litro de _____

9 un paquete de _____

10 un trozo de _____

11 un tubo de _____

12 un cuarto de _____

Q Look in the kitchen cupboard. How many containers and items can you name in Spanish?

PRACTICE

Remember
For single items, use <u>no queda</u> (there's none left). For plural ones, use <u>no quedan</u> (there are none left).

Q How do you explain 'you have no coins left'?

Practise this dialogue with a friend. Then use the suggestions on the right to make up another conversation by changing the underlined words.

Empleado/a: Buenos días, señor(a). ¿Qué desea?

Tú: Quisiera <u>un kilo de manzanas</u>, por favor.

Empleado/a: Muy bien. ¿Algo más?

Tú: Sí. Deme <u>una lata de sardinas</u> y <u>una botella de vino</u>.

Empleado/a: Aquí tiene. ¿Es todo?

Tú: ¿Tiene <u>pan</u>?

Empleado/a: Lo siento, no queda(n).

Tú: Es todo, entonces. ¿Cuánto es?

Empleado/a: Son <u>catorce</u> euros <u>cincuenta</u> céntimos.

Tú: Lo siento, no tengo cambio. Sólo tengo un billete de <u>cien</u> euros.

Empleado/a: No importa. Aquí tiene.

Tú: Gracias. Adiós.

Empleado/a: De nada. Adiós.

1k bananas
tin of tomatoes
bottle of lemonade
grapes?
only got 50 euro note
(Total: 7.50 euros.)

If you have to ask in the role-play how much the shopping comes to, use either ¿cuánto es en total? (how much is it altogether?), or ¿cuánto le debo? (how much do I owe you?).

A Contacting others

Remember
When answering the phone, it's usual to say ¡Diga! or ¡Dígame! The person who's calling will then say ¡Oiga!

¡Diga!/¡Dígame!	Hello!
¡Oiga! ¿Está ...? ¿Me pone(s) con ... ?	Hello! Is ... there? Can I speak to ... ?
¿De parte de quién? De parte de	Who's speaking? It's ... .
Está comunicando. No contesta.	The line is engaged. It's not answering.
¿Cuál es el número/prefijo?	What's the number/dialing code?
¿Qué número hay que marcar?	What number do you have to dial?
¿Puedo dejar un recado?	Can I leave a message?

la cabina	public telephone	la línea, la llamada	the line, the call
colgar	to hang up	el teléfono movil	mobile phone
la guia telefónica	phone book	el correo electrónico	e-mail

B Part-time jobs

Remember
When describing what happened repeatedly over a period of time, use the imperfect tense: Trabajaba en una oficina. (I worked in an office.)

¿Tienes algún empleo? – ¿Cuándo trabajas?	Do you have a job? When do you work?
Trabajo todos los días, el fin de semana, desde las ... hasta las ...	I work every day, at the weekend, from ... until ...
¿Cuántas horas trabajas? – Trabajo ...	How many hours do you work? – I work ...
¿Cuándo empiezas? – ¿Cuándo terminas?	When do you start? – When do you finish?
¿Cuánto ganas? – Gano ...	How much do you earn? – I earn ...
¿Qué opinas del trabajo? – Es (aburrido).	What do you think about work? – It's (boring).

interesante	interesting	duro, dificil, fácil	hard, difficult, easy
pesado, útil	boring, useful	rutinario, repetitivo	routine, repetitive
agradable	pleasant	bien/mal pagado	well/badly paid

C Work experience

¿Dónde hiciste tu experiencia laboral?	Where did you do your work experience?
La hice en ... /Trabajé en ...	I did it in .../I worked in ...
¿Cuánto tiempo duró? – Duró ... días.	How long did it last? – It lasted ... days.
¿Cómo ibas a tu lugar de trabajo?	How did you get to your workplace?
Iba andando, en tren, en autobús.	I used to go on foot, by train, by bus.
¿Cuánto tiempo tardabas en llegar?	How long did it take to get there?
Tardaba unos (20) minutos.	It took/used to take about (20) minutes.
¿Cómo era el horario?	What was your timetable like?
Empezaba/terminaba a las (nueve).	I began/I finished at (nine).
¿Qué tenías que hacer?	What did you have to do?
Tenía que (archivar, coger el teléfono).	I had to (do the filing, answer the phone).

D The imperfect tense

The imperfect tense describes what something was like, what was happening, or what used to happen. For regular verbs, remove the –ar, –er, –ir from the infinitive, and add these endings:

	–ar hablar *(to speak)*	–er beber *(to drink)*	–ir vivir *(to live)*
yo	hablaba	bebía	vivía
tú	hablabas	bebías	vivías
él, ella, usted	hablaba	bebía	vivía
nosotros	hablábamos	bebíamos	vivíamos
vosotros	hablábais	bebíais	vivíais
ellos, ellas, ustedes	hablaban	bebían	vivían

IR *(to go)*	iba, ibas, iba, íbamos, ibais, iban
SER *(to be)*	era, eras, era, éramos, erais, eran
VER *(to see)*	veía, veías, veía, veíamos, veíais, veían

Vivíamos en la costa. Era tranquilo. Iba a la playa. Había mucha gente. Hacía buen tiempo.	*We used to live on the coast. It was quiet. I used to go to the beach. There were a lot of people. The weather was good.*

1 Put the verbs in brackets into the imperfect tense.

Ejemplo: (ir) – iba

> Hice mi experiencia laboral en la oficina de un arquitecto, igual que mi amigo Juan. Yo (ir) al trabajo andando, porque la oficina no (estar) muy lejos de casa, pero él (tomar) el autobús. Nosotros (empezar) a las nueve, pero los otros empleados (tener) que estar allí a las ocho. Me (gustar) el trabajo: yo (archivar) primero, o (hacer) recados, y Juan (coger) el teléfono y (repartir) el correo. En la hora de comer, nosotros (soler) ir al bar de enfrente.

E The gerund and continuous tenses

The gerund in English ends in -ing, e.g. walking, reading. It's often used with while, when, by: when walking to school ... while eating ... by writing ... Form it like this:

-ar verbs	*remove* -ar	-ando	*add* andar - andando *(walking)*
-er verbs	*remove* -er	-iendo	*add* comer - comiendo *(eating)*
-ir verbs	*remove* -ir	-iendo	*add* escribir - escribiendo *(writing)*

The present continuous indicates what you are doing right now (I'm studying) and the imperfect tense describes what you were doing (I was watching TV when ...). Use the present or imperfect tense of the verb estar (p.) and the gerund.

¿Yo? Estoy haciendo mis deberes. Cuando llegué, María estaba planchando.	*Me? I'm doing my homework. When I arrived, María was ironing.*

Phoning and travelling

THE BARE BONES
➤ Leave or respond to phone messages.
➤ Give, understand and ask for information about travel to work.

Remember

Spanish phone numbers are given in pairs: 54 20 12 is <u>cincuenta y cuatro</u>, <u>veinte</u>, <u>doce</u>. Where there is a group of three at the start (e.g. 430), the first one is given on its own: <u>cuatro</u>, <u>treinta</u> ... !

Remember

To express anger or disappointment, you can use ¡Qué pena!, ¡Qué fastidio!, ¡Qué lata!

Q How would you say your own phone number, or that of a friend, in Spanish?

A Phone messages

1 You may hear, or have to give, a **phone message**.

2 Revise **useful phrases** by doing the activity below.

<u>Empareja a–h con 1–8.</u> **Match a–h with 1–8.**

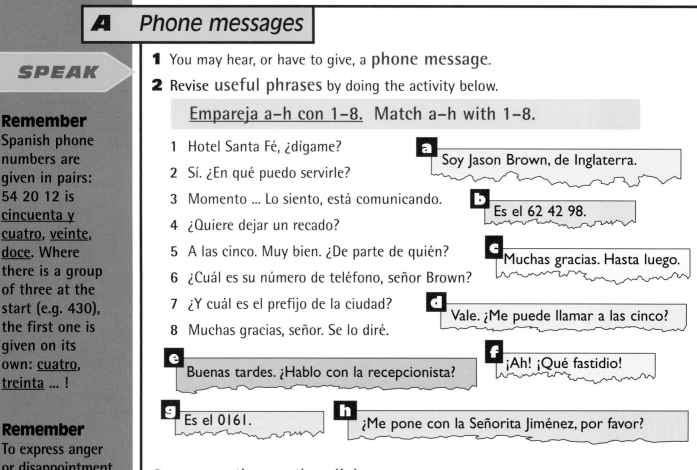

1 Hotel Santa Fé, ¿dígame?

2 Sí. ¿En qué puedo servirle?

3 Momento ... Lo siento, está comunicando.

4 ¿Quiere dejar un recado?

5 A las cinco. Muy bien. ¿De parte de quién?

6 ¿Cuál es su número de teléfono, señor Brown?

7 ¿Y cuál es el prefijo de la ciudad?

8 Muchas gracias, señor. Se lo diré.

a Soy Jason Brown, de Inglaterra.

b Es el 62 42 98.

c Muchas gracias. Hasta luego.

d Vale. ¿Me puede llamar a las cinco?

e Buenas tardes. ¿Hablo con la recepcionista?

f ¡Ah! ¡Qué fastidio!

g Es el 0161.

h ¿Me pone con la Señorita Jiménez, por favor?

3 Now **practise another dialogue**: the receptionist's replies remain mostly the same, but you need to **give the following information**:

• Ask if you're talking to the secretary.

• Ask to be put through to Sr. Gómez.

• Express your annoyance.

• Ask him to call you at half-past-four.

• Explain you're Sam Thompson, from Wales.

• Give her your phone number: 740692.

• Give her the code: 01745.

• Say 'thank you' and 'good bye'.

B Means of travel

With shorter texts, you may need to understand only one or two key words.

You may have to **match up sentences and pictures**.

1 First, **study the pictures** carefully – what do they show?

2 What word(s) do(es) each one suggest to you?

Escribe la letra correcta en cada casilla.
Write the correct letter in each box.

1 Semana de la Salud, mayo 7–14: ¡venid al instituto a pie! ☐
2 ¿Te interesa visitar Gran Bretaña? octubre 15-22, viaje en avión. ☐
3 Autocar Centro-Río Rosas. Salida 14.40. ☐
4 ¡Perdido! Permiso de tren. Ana Vallejas 1°EGB ☐
5 ¡Si vienes en moto, hay que llevar casco! ☐
6 Nuevo – soporte para bicicletas, detrás del gimnasio. ☐

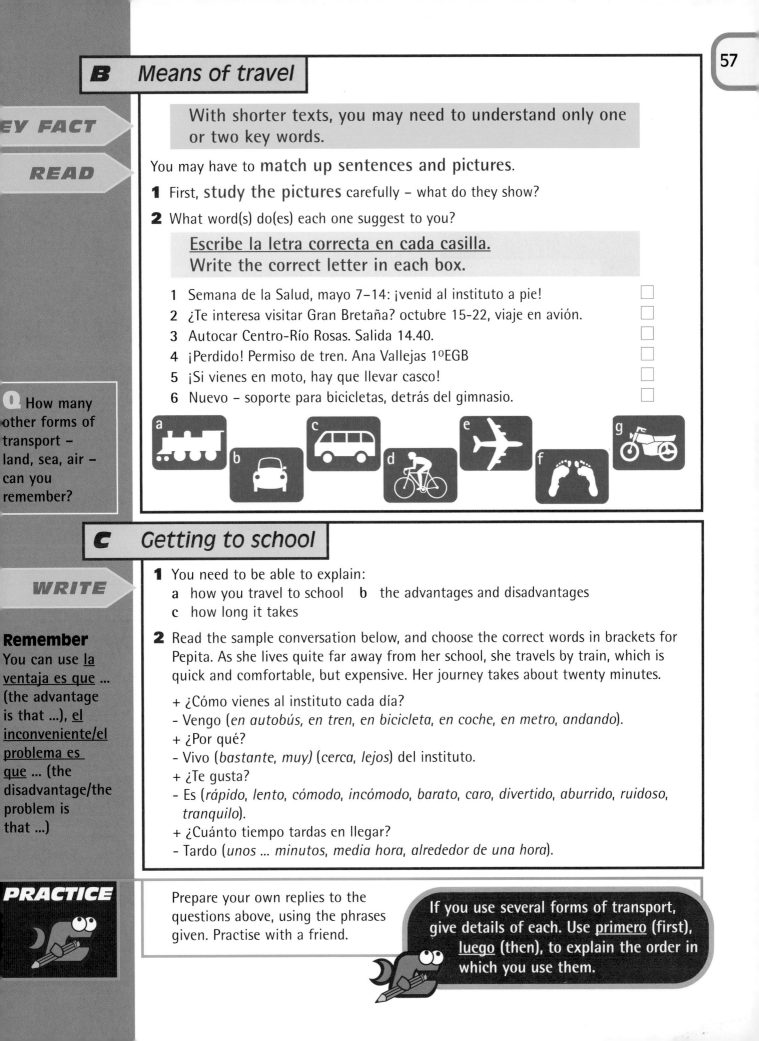

Q How many other forms of transport – land, sea, air – can you remember?

C Getting to school

1 You need to be able to explain:
a how you travel to school   b   the advantages and disadvantages
c how long it takes

2 Read the sample conversation below, and choose the correct words in brackets for Pepita. As she lives quite far away from her school, she travels by train, which is quick and comfortable, but expensive. Her journey takes about twenty minutes.

+ ¿Cómo vienes al instituto cada día?
- Vengo (*en autobús, en tren, en bicicleta, en coche, en metro, andando*).
+ ¿Por qué?
- Vivo (*bastante, muy*) (*cerca, lejos*) del instituto.
+ ¿Te gusta?
- Es (*rápido, lento, cómodo, incómodo, barato, caro, divertido, aburrido, ruidoso, tranquilo*).
+ ¿Cuánto tiempo tardas en llegar?
- Tardo (*unos ... minutos, media hora, alrededor de una hora*).

Remember
You can use <u>la ventaja es que ...</u> (the advantage is that ...), <u>el inconveniente/el problema es que ...</u> (the disadvantage/the problem is that ...)

PRACTICE

Prepare your own replies to the questions above, using the phrases given. Practise with a friend.

If you use several forms of transport, give details of each. Use <u>primero</u> (first), <u>luego</u> (then), to explain the order in which you use them.

Part-time jobs

➤ Give and understand information about part-time jobs.
➤ Explain what you spend money on.

A Part-time jobs

READ

Remember
Remember matching tasks like this always have more possible answers than questions. You will need to read carefully to work out which ones do not apply.

Q How would you reply to questions 1–7?

1 In the speaking part of the exam, you may be asked if you have a **part-time job**, or **work in the holidays**.

2 You will need to **answer questions** about **what you do, your hours, how much you earn** and **what you think of it**.

<u>Para cada pregunta 1–7, escribe la letra de la respuesta apropiada.</u> For each question 1–7, write the letter of the appropriate reply.

1 ¿Tienes algún empleo?	a Siete horas en total.
2 ¿Cuándo trabajas?	b Mis padres no me dejan trabajar.
3 ¿Cuántas horas trabajas?	c Sí, en un garaje.
4 ¿Cuándo empiezas?	d A las cuatro de la tarde.
5 ¿Cuándo terminas?	e Siete euros por hora.
6 ¿Cuánto ganas?	f Los sábados.
7 ¿Qué opinas del trabajo?	g Es interesante. Aprendo mucho.
	h A las nueve de la mañana.

B Expanding your replies

KEY FACT

SPEAK

Remember
In the conversation part of the exam, the more your voice is heard, the more marks you can get. Don't leave it up to your teacher to do all the talking!

Use verbs in your replies. Say as much as you can.

1 In the replies a–h above, there are few verbs. Use a verb in each sentence: **trabajo** (I work), **empiezo** (I begin), **termino** (I finish), **gano** (I earn).

2 Use the information above to fill in the gaps below.

<u>Rellena los espacios.</u> Fill in the gaps.

¿Tienes algún empleo?
Sí. Trabajo en un garaje los ...(1)... . Trabajo ...(2)... horas normalmente: empiezo a las ...(3)... de la mañana, y termino a las ...(4)... de la tarde, en general.

¿Cuánto ganas?
Gano ...(5)... por hora. No está mal, y me gusta el trabajo. Es duro y aburrido a veces, pero en general es ...(6)... .

C How you spend your money

READ

1 Reading texts and questions often contain **'false trails'**: similar words or expressions **which can mislead** unless you read other words around them carefully.

2 Each question 1–7 below has a 'false trail'. **Read the following tips** to help with the first three questions.

Q1 contains the word **numerosa**, and text 1 has the numbers **dos** and **cinco**: don't be misled!

Q2 The word **deportista** comes up in text 3, but are there any negatives near it? Who else does sport?

Q3 The expression **fin de semana** appears in text 3, but is it in the context of weekend work?

> **Escribe el nombre de la persona más apropiada.**
> Write the name of the most appropriate person.

¿Recibes dinero? ¿Cuánto? ¿Cuándo?

1 Mi madrastra es enfermera, y tiene que trabajar mucho. ¡Yo también! Cuido a mis hermanas (de dos y cinco años) los sábados y los domingos. Casi todo el dinero que gano lo uso para pagarme cursos de piragüismo.

ISABEL

2 No me dan mucho dinero mis padres porque somos seis hermanas en total. Y no trabajo fuera de casa: tengo examenes en junio. Cada noche tengo un montón de deberes – ¡demasiados!

SABRINA

3 Yo gano dinero trabajando en un garaje, de lunes a viernes. Empiezo a las seis de la tarde y termino a las diez. Gasto mi dinero en CDs y revistas. No salgo mucho el fin de semana – estudio un poco – y no soy nada deportista.

PABLO

4 Mis padres me dan setenta euros al mes. Parece mucho, pero tengo que pagar todo: la ropa, los libros, las diversiones, aún los viajes en autobús para ir al instituto – ¡eso no es justo! A finales del mes, ¡no tengo ni un euro!

ENRIQUE

Q What does Isabel's step-mother do? Why is June an important month for Sabrina? How many hours a week does Pablo work? What does Enrique think is unfair?

1 ¿Quién es miembro de una familia numerosa? _____
2 ¿Quién es deportista? _____
3 ¿Quién tiene que trabajar el fin de semana? _____
4 ¿Quién gasta todo su dinero? _____
5 ¿Quién tiene que estudiar mucho? _____
6 ¿Quién no recibe dinero de sus padres? _____
7 ¿Quién prefiere quedarse en casa los fines de semana? _____

PRACTICE

Answer the following questions in Spanish:

1 ¿Tienes algún empleo?
2 ¿Qué haces? ¿Dónde trabajas?
3 ¿Cómo es el horario?
4 ¿Cuánto dinero ganas/recibes?
5 ¿En qué gastas tu dinero?

> If you don't have a part-time job, you can either invent one, or explain what you would like to do: <u>me gustaría trabajar/ganar/gastar mi dinero en</u> … .
> (I would like to work/earn/spend my money on … .)

Work experience

➤ Talk and write about your work experience.
➤ This topic provides a good opportunity for using a range of tenses.

A Work experience

READ

1 In the conversation part of the exam, you may have to **give details about your work experience**: called either **la experiencia laboral or las prácticas de trabajo**.

2 Start off by matching the questions 1–8 below with their Spanish equivalents a–h in the conversation at the bottom of the page.

Ejemplo: 1 e

1 What were your hours like?
2 How did you get to work?
3 When was the lunch break?
4 Where did you do your work experience?

5 Were there any breaks?
6 How long did it take to get there?
7 Did you like the work?
8 How long did your work experience last?

B Giving details

SPEAK

1 Even if the work was repetitive (**repetitivo**) or your boss was a pain (**mi jefe/a era pesado/a**), your work mates were probably nice (**mis compañeros eran simpáticos**)!

> **Practica la conversación siguiente. Inventa otra e utiliza los apuntes en inglés.** Practise the following conversation. Invent another one using the notes in English.

Remember
Try and use some of the following expressions to add colour and variety to what you say: para decir la verdad (to tell the truth), francamente (frankly), en realidad (in fact), en general (on the whole) or a veces/de vez en cuando (sometimes).

a *¿Dónde hiciste tu experiencia laboral?* – Trabajé en un laboratorio.
b *¿Cuánto tiempo duraron las prácticas?* – Duraron quince días.
c *¿Cómo ibas a tu trabajo?* – Iba en metro.
d *¿Cuánto tiempo tardabas en llegar?* – Tardaba unos treinta minutos.
e *¿Cómo era tu horario?* – Trabajaba desde las ocho hasta las cuatro.
f *¿Había descansos?* – Sí. Había dos descansos de quince minutos.
g *¿Cuándo era la hora de comer?* – Era de doce a una.
h *¿Te gustaba el trabajo?* – Sí. En general, era bastante interesante pero a veces era aburrido.

> **Work experience:** 10 days in travel agents. Went by bus and on foot – took nearly an hour! Hours: 9–5.30, with lunch from 1–2. Breaks: 3 x 20 mins. Great fun on the whole, but a bit repetitive sometimes.

C Presentations

Remember
You can't read from your notes when giving a presentation, but you are allowed several postcard-sized pieces of paper with a few headings in Spanish on each one to prompt you.

Q Write a sentence or two, expressing your opinion of your work experience. Use the phrases on page 54 to help.

Use a range of tenses to be eligible for high marks.

1 As part of the exam, you will have to give a **presentation** on a topic of your choice.

2 The world of work can be a good one to choose because you can use a **range of tenses**.

3 To prepare for your presentation, make written notes on the following topic headings. Where it says (infin.) you will need to use an infinitive, for example, **suelo trabajar** (*I usually work*).

Present tense
- trabajo – *I work*
- empiezo – *I start*
- termino – *I finish*
- gano – *I earn*
- me gusta – *I like*
- suelo (infin.) – *I usually*

Past tense
- trabajé – *I worked*
- fui allí – *I went there*
- empezaba – *I started*
- terminaba – *I finished*
- tenía que (infin.) – *I had to*
- me gustaba – *I liked*

Future tense
- voy a (infin.) – *I'm going to*
- tengo la intención de (infin.) – *I plan to*
- quisiera (infin.) – *I'd like to*
- iré – *I will go*
- espero (infin.) – *I hope to*
- pienso (infin.) – *I'm thinking of*

PRACTICE

Answer these questions in Spanish.

¡Hola! Me llamo Manolo. De lunes a viernes, trabajo en una frutería cerca de casa. Es aburrido pero gano bastante. El otoño pasado, hice mis prácticas de trabajo en una oficina de información y turismo, y me divertí mucho. Tenía que tratar con el público, lo que me gustaba mucho, pero mejor todavía era preparar folletos turísticos en el ordenador. Después de los exámenes hay la posibilidad de tener un empleo en la misma oficina, pero quiero seguir estudiando el año próximo. También quisiera viajar al extranjero – el año pasado, fui a México con mi familia y tal vez un día iré a vivir en otro país sudamericano como Bolivia.

1 ¿Dónde trabajó Manolo el año pasado?
2 ¿Qué opina de su empleo actual?
3 ¿Qué le gustó más de su experiencia laboral?
4 ¿Qué va a hacer después de los exámenes?
5 ¿Cuál es la ventaja de trabajar en la frutería?
6 ¿Qué país espera visitar?

It is vital to recognise present, past and future tenses for this task – otherwise you may give the wrong information.

Vocabulary

A Character

De carácter, ¿cómo eres? – Soy ...	What is your personality like? – I'm ...
¿Cómo es tu (padre/madre)?	What's your (father/mother) like?
¿Cuáles son las características de ...	What are the characteristics of ...
un bueno amigo/una buena amiga?	a good friend?
Él/ella debe ser ...	He/she should be ...

afable	*pleasant*	gracioso/a	*funny, witty*
amistoso/a	*friendly*	hablador/a	*talkative*
atento/a	*polite, attentive*	honrado/a	*honest*
atrevido/a	*daring, bold*	introvertido/a	*introverted*
cariñoso/a	*affectionate*	mal educado/a	*rude*
celoso/a	*jealous*	mentiroso/a	*liar*
chistoso/a	*jokey, funny*	mezquino/a	*mean, stingy*
cobarde	*cowardly*	orgulloso/a	*proud*
comprensivo/a	*understanding*	perezoso/a	*lazy*
cortés	*polite*	seguro/a de sí mismo/a	*confident*
cuidadoso/a	*careful*	sensible	*sensitive*
egoísta	*selfish, egotistic(al)*	sensato/a	*sensible*
emprendedor/a	*enterprising*	serio/a	*serious*
encantador/a	*charming, delightful*	severo/a	*severe*
extrovertido	*extrovert, out-going*	torpe	*clumsy*
formal	*reliable, serious*	travieso/a	*naughty*
goloso/a	*greedy*	valiente	*brave*

B Relationships

¿Te llevas bien con (tu hermano)?	Do you get on well with (your brother)?
Me llevo bien con .../no me llevo bien con ...	I get on well with .../I don't get on well with ...
Mi (hermana) me irrita, me fastidia,	My (sister) irritates me, annoys me,
me hace subir por las paredes,	drives me up the wall,
me pone malo/a, me vuelve loco/a.	makes me ill, makes me mad/angry.
Me enfado con él, ella, mi (hermana).	I get angry with him, her, my (sister).
Su comportamiento es bueno.	His/her behaviour is good.
Su conducta es mala.	His/her behaviour is bad.
Las relaciones son buenas/malas.	Relations are good/bad.

normalmente	*usually*	hay disputas	*there are arguments*
a veces	*sometimes*	estar ...	*to be ...*
en general	*generally*	de buen humor	*in a good mood*
tener confianza (en)	*to trust*	de mal humor	*in a bad mood*
tener orgullo (de)	*to be proud (of)*	enamorado/a	*in love*
el sentido común	*common sense*	decepcionado/a	*disappointed*

C Environment

¿Qué debemos hacer ...	*What should we do ...*		
para proteger el medio ambiente?	*to protect the environment?*		
(No) debemos/deberíamos (utilizar) ...	*We must/should (not) (use) ...*		
vidrio, papel, bolsas de plástico, agua	*glass, paper, plastic bags, water*		
Debe haber más/menos ...	*There ought to be more/less, fewer ...*		
Me preocupo por .../me inquieto por ...	*I'm worried about .../I get upset about ...*		
la contaminación/la polución	*pollution*		

sería mejor ...	*it would be better ...*	estropear	*to spoil, damage*
reducir, reciclar	*to reduce, to recycle*	contaminar	*to contaminate*
utilizar, reutilizar	*to use, to reuse*	matar, arder	*to kill, to burn*
ahorrar, gastar	*to save, to waste*	podría ser .../es ...	*it could be .../it is ...*
consumir, salvar	*to consume, to save*	dañoso, ecológico	*harmful, ecological*
producir, evitar	*to produce, to avoid*	desastroso	*disastrous*
arruinar, amenazar	*to ruin, to threaten*	imprudente	*short-sighted*
controlar, destruir	*to control, to destroy*	peligroso	*dangerous*

el aire, el mar	*air, sea*	la marea negra	*oil slick*
el atasco	*traffic jam*	la naturaleza	*nature*
la basura	*rubbish*	el planeta	*planet*
la circulación	*traffic*	el recurso natural	*natural resource*
el desastre	*disaster*	el reciclaje	*recycling*
la destrucción	*destruction*	la selva, la tierra	*jungle, earth*
la ecología	*ecology*	la sequía	*drought*
la energía	*energy*	el tráfico	*traffic*
la extinción	*extinction*	el vehículo	*vehicle*
el gasóleo	*petrol*	la urbanización	*housing estate*
sin plomo	*unleaded*	la vivienda	*housing, house*
la gasolina	*diesel (oil)*	la capa de ozono	*ozone layer*
la inundación	*flood*	el contenador	*container*

D Education issues

¿Adónde quieres ir ...	*Where do you want to go ...*		
para seguir tus/sus estudios?	*to continue your studies?*		
Quiero/Espero ir a ...	*I want to/I hope to go to ...*		
una academia, la universidad	*an academy, university*		
hacer una carrera en ...	*to do a university course in ...*		
¿Qué opinas de tener reglas/normas?	*What do you think about having rules?*		
¿Estás a favor del uniforme?	*Are you in favour of uniform?*		

tener la opción de	*to have the option to*	castigar, obedecer	*to punish, to obey*
tener prácticas en	*to have training in*	el castigo	*punishment*
los deberes	*the duties*	desobedecer	*to disobey*
los derechos	*the rights*	respetar	*to respect*
obligatorio	*compulsory*	riguroso	*strict, stringent*

Grammar

A The future and conditional tenses

Remember
The future of
<u>hay</u> (there is/are)
is <u>habrá</u>, and the
conditional is
<u>habría</u>.

The future tense indicates what will happen. The conditional indicates what would happen. You will notice that the endings are added to the infinitive. They are the same for all three verb types: –ar, –er, –ir.

	FUTURE	CONDITIONAL
	–ar (hablar)	–ar (hablar)
yo	hablar**é**	hablar**ía**
tú	hablar**ás**	hablar**ías**
él, ella, usted	hablar**á**	hablar**ía**
nosotros	hablar**emos**	hablar**íamos**
vosotros	hablar**éis**	hablar**íais**
ellos, ellas, ustedes	hablar**án**	hablar**ían**

Hablaré con el gerente mañana.	*I will speak to the manager tomorrow.*
Comeremos en la terraza.	*We will eat on the terrace.*
¿Dónde vivirías?	*Where would you live?*
¿Qué tipo de trabajo te gustaría?	*What sort of work would you like?*

The following verbs have irregular stems in both the future and the conditional. They have regular endings:

INFINITIVE		STEM	INFINITIVE		STEM
to say	decir	dir–	*to know*	saber	sabr–
to do, make	hacer	har–	*to go out*	salir	saldr–
to be able to	poder	podr–	*to have*	tener	tendr–
to put, lay, set	poner	pondr–	*to come*	venir	vendr–
to want to	querer	querr–	*to be worth*	valer	valdr–

Lo haré pasado mañana.	*I will do it the day after tomorrow.*
Tendrá que ir a Inglaterra en mayo.	*He will have to go to England in May.*
Querríamos viajar si posible.	*We would like to travel, if possible.*
Podría ir a la universidad.	*I would be able to go to university.*

1 Put the underlined verbs into the future tense, and the verbs in brackets into the conditional.

> ¿El instituto del futuro? Creo que <u>tiene</u> menos alumnos jóvenes y más adultos. Todo el mundo <u>aprende</u> en centros de información, y no en aulas. <u>Hay</u> más ordenadores y <u>es</u> posible quedarse en casa. Si posible, yo (ir) sólo un día o dos a la semana, y (poder) estudiar una gama más grande de asignaturas. (Querer) visitar más países, (hacer) más prácticas de trabajo ¡y no (haber) tantos exámenes!

B Relative pronouns

Relative pronouns link parts of a sentence together.

que who, that, which	La chica que vive allí. La casa, que es nueva ... *The girl who lives there. The house, that is new ...*
quién(es) who, whom	No sé quién vive allí. *I don't know who lives there.*
lo que what (that which)	No sé lo que quiere Marta. *I don't know what Marta wants.*

2 Complete each sentence with the correct relative pronoun.

a Mi hermano, _____ se llama Santi, tiene dieciocho años.
b Creo que tiene una novia, pero no sé _____ es.
c Santi dice que no le interesan las chicas, ¡ _____ no es verdad!
d A lo mejor, es la chica guapa _____ vive enfrente.
e Santi pasa horas mirando por la ventana, _____ me hace sospechar.

C Ser/estar

Both **ser** and **estar** mean 'to be', but are used in different contexts:

SER	ESTAR
Permanent characteristics E.g. Es simpático. *(He's nice.)*	Temporary states E.g. El té está caliente. *(The tea is hot.)*
Jobs, professions E.g. Soy enfermera. *(I'm a nurse.)*	Feelings, moods E.g. Estoy deprimido. *(I'm depressed.)*
Time E.g. Es la una. *(It's one o'clock.)*	Position, place E.g. Está a la izquierda. *(It's on the left.)*

D Negative commands

To instruct someone NOT to do something, take the **yo** form of the present tense, remove the final **-o**, and add these endings:

	TÚ	VOSOTROS	USTED	USTEDES
-ar hablo	no hables	no habléis	no hable	no hablen
-er como	no comas	no comáis	no coma	no coman
-ir escribo	no escribas	no escribáis	no escriba	no escriban

This holds true if the **yo** form is irregular: e.g. **salir (yo salgo)**, **poner (yo pongo)**.

| Señor, no hable tan rápido. ¡No comáis chicle! ¡No salgas, Marta, por favor! ¡No ponga el libro allí! | *Sir, do not talk so fast.* *Don't eat chewing-gum!* *Don't go out, Marta, please!* *Don't put the book there!* |

Personal relationships

➤ Talk about your own personality.
➤ Talk about relationships with others.

A Character

KEY FACT

Now is the time to work out what you want to say. You will not have time to think about it in the exam.

WRITE

1 You need to be able to describe yourself, and members of your family or a friend.

2 With adjectives of character, use the verb ser: soy/es ... (*I am/he is, she is ...*)

Remember
When describing a female, the adjective needs to be female. Adjectives ending in -e do not change; those ending in -o change to -a; those ending in a consonant add an -a.

Busca las parejas. Match up the opposites.

Ejemplo: 1 amable – 5 cruel

1 amable	11 insincero/a
2 mezquino/a	12 insolente
3 antipático/a	13 inteligente
4 cortés	14 nervioso/a
5 cruel	15 obediente
6 desobediente	16 paciente
7 estúpido/a	17 seguro/a de sí mismo/a
8 extrovertido	18 simpático
9 generoso/a	19 sincero/a
10 impaciente	20 tímido/a

B Getting on with others — or not!

KEY FACT

Be prepared to talk about your relationships.

1 Learn two or three useful phrases from page 62.

SPEAK

2 You can use them in writing, or in speaking.

Q Can you answer the questions so that they are true for you. Alter hermana to hermano or amigo/a, whichever is more appropriate for you.

Contesta a las preguntas. Answers the questions.

¿Te llevas bien con tu hermana?
(*Explain that you don't get on with her.*)
¿Qué pasa?
(*Say that she annoys you, and you get angry with her.*)
¿Te llevas bien con tus padres?
(*Explain that there are arguments sometimes but in general relationships are good.*)
¿Cuáles son las características de una buena amiga?
(*Say what characteristics you think a good friend should have.*)

C Moods and feelings

READ

1 With adjectives of **mood and feeling**, use the verb **estar** (*to be*): **estoy ...** (*I am ...*).

> ¿ Cada adjetivo indica un humor positivo (P) o negativo (N)? Does each adjective indicate a positive mood (P) or a negative one (N)?
>
> deprimido/a triste ilusionado/a estresado/a enfadado/a
> contento/a preocupado/a furioso/a cansado/a harto/a

2 In the following type of task, you have to **choose the correct summary** for each person.

3 With each text, first work out **which summaries will not apply**. In the remaining ones, **pay attention to smaller details**: where, when, and with whom.

> Escoge el resumen correcto A–E para cada persona.
> Choose the correct summary A–E for each person.

A Se lleva bien con su hermana.
B No le gusta mucho su hermana.
C Su hermana se comporta mal en el instituto.
D Se enfada con su hermana.
E Su hermana es muy generosa.

1 ¿Mi hermana? Coge mis cosas, saca dinero de mi monedero, entra en mi cuarto sin pedir permiso... A veces, me pongo furiosa con ella.

2 Es muy segura de sí misma en casa, pero siempre quiere tener razón, y es agresiva también – hay muchas disputas entre ella y sus compañeros de clase.

3 Mi hermana es cariñosa y amistosa con mi hermano mayor. Yo no tengo esta suerte – se comporta muy mal conmigo. Es mentirosa, y mezquina. La odio.

Remember

Words like <u>pero</u> (but) and <u>sin embargo</u> (nevertheless) indicate that something different will be expressed afterwards.

Q How do you feel in the following situations? Begin with <u>Estoy</u> (I am) or <u>Me siento</u> (I feel): a) <u>el viernes después de las clases</u>; b) <u>antes de un examen</u>; c) <u>el lunes por la mañana</u>.

PRACTICE

Write a short paragraph in Spanish describing important people in your life – parents, brothers and sisters, friends, or teachers – and how you get on with them. Use the adjectives of character, mood and feeling, and expressions that indicate your relationships with others.

It is not necessary to write a long list of adjectives of character or mood in the exam: use a range of expressions to show what you know.

The environment

➤ Give and understand opinions about pollution and the environment.
➤ Understand and discuss wider issues: e.g. transport, wildlife, energy sources.

A Improving the environment

KEY FACT

This is a good topic in which to use the conditional tense.

WRITE

1 You need to be able to **talk and write about the environment**.

2 What do you think we **should do**, or **shouldn't do**:

  a) **within the home** environment?

  b) **in the street** – in what we buy, use or throw away?

  c) **in general**, to protect our environment?

3 Use the grids below to help you work out what you want to say.

Remember
Tanto (as/so much, as/so many) is an adjective. It must be the same gender (masculine, feminine) and number (singular, plural) as the noun it describes: tanto vidrio (as/so much glass), tantas bolsas (as/so many bags).

Escribe tres frases para exprimir tu opinion con la ayuda de los cuadros. Write three sentences to express your opinion. Use the grids to help you.

Ejemplo: En el hogar, deberíamos ahorrar más agua, y no debemos utilizar tantos contenedores de plástico.

A En el hogar ...	B En la calle ...	C En general ...
In the home	In the street	In general

(No)	debemos	utilizar, reutilizar, reciclar, ahorrar
	deberíamos	gastar, tirar, echar, comprar, consumir
	sería mejor	producir, reducir la cantidad de ...

más/menos	tanto	vidrio, papel, plástico, gasóleo
	tanta	agua, ropa, gasolina, basura
	tantos	contenadores, recursos naturales
	tantas	bolsas (de plástico)

Q How would you say: 'We should not use as many natural resources, like petrol, electricity and coal (el carbón)', for example?

B Transport issues

EY FACT

READ

You will not usually be expected to write more than a few words.

1 In the reading exam, you may have to write answers in Spanish.

2 There may be a word, or words, in the text which you can reuse in your answer.

3 You may need to use the verb form of a noun given in the text, or vice-versa.

4 Use the following hints to help:

Leonora: After <u>de</u>, you will need a noun or a verb.

Adriano: After <u>es</u>, you will need an adjective here.

Paco: After <u>se puede</u>, you will need a verb.

Remember
There may be words you don't know in the reading texts. Unfamiliar but important words will have an English explanation.

<u>Completa las frases en español.</u>
Complete the sentences in Spanish.

En el centro nuevo de mi ciudad, hay calles anchas para los coches, y se puede circular fácilmente. Pero hay mucho tráfico en los barrios más antiguos, donde suele haber atascos.

Leonora

En mi ciudad, necesitamos una red*de transporte público más eficiente pero también más barata. Muchos jóvenes no tienen bastante dinero para pagar los billetes.

Adriano

* red = *network*

Ahora que tengo mi carnet de conducir, puedo ir al centro comercial nuevo sin problemas. Hay muchos aparcamientos, y son gratis también.

Paco

Leonora: En el centro, no hay problemas de ....

Adriano: El problema para los jóvenes es que el transporte es ....

Paco: Lo bueno es que se puede .... fácilmente.

Q What are the nouns from the verbs <u>aparcar</u> (to park), and <u>circular</u> (to move around)?

PRACTICE

How might you answer the following questions in the speaking part of the exam?

¿Cómo se puede proteger el medio ambiente?
(How can we protect the environment?)
¿Cómo se puede mejorar tu ciudad?
(How could your town be improved?)
En tu/su opinión, ¿cuáles son los problemas del medio ambiente más importantes?
(In your opinion, which are the most important issues as regards the environment?)

As well as your opinion, you can add expressions which indicate your feelings: <u>me inquieto por</u> ... (I'm anxious about ...), <u>me preocupo por</u> ... (I'm worried about ...).

Education issues

THE BARE BONES

➤ Prepare your thoughts on school issues: e.g. rules, uniform, benefits.

➤ Ensure you can talk or write about your choices of study and training.

A School: the good and the bad

KEY FACT

It is possible to find simple ways of explaining complex ideas: many expressions are similar to English ones.

SPEAK

1 You may be asked to **give your opinion** on different aspects of **school life.**

2 Choose the replies which **most closely reflect your views** from the alternatives below. Adapt them if you like.

Elige la respuesta más apropiada para ti.
Choose the reply which is most appropriate for you.

¿Qué opinas de las reglas en tu instituto?
1 Creo que las reglas son ...
• necesarias.
• demasiadas severas.
• estúpidas.

¿Por qué?
2 Las reglas existen para ...
• ayudarte a respetar los derechos de los demás.
• limitar tu libertad de expresión.
• fastidiar a los alumnos.

¿Hay algo que cambiarías?
3 Cambiaría las normas sobre ...
• el uniforme: sería mejor llevar lo que quieres.
• las asignaturas que se puede estudiar.
• el castigo: no es justo.

¿Qué opinas de la disciplina en tu instituto?
4 Creo que ...
• es buena: la mayoría de los alumnos trabajan bien.
• es mala: hay mucha gente que no se comportan bien.
• puede ser mejor: hay intimidación de algunos alumnos por otros.

¿Cuáles son las ventajas de ir al instituto?
5 La ventaja más grande es que ...
• sales con buenas calificaciones.
• aprendes a relacionarte con muchas personas diferentes.
• puedes probar muchas asignaturas diferentes.

Remember
Many Spanish words ending in -ción end in -tion in English, e.g. atención, educación, acción.

Q What do you think the following words mean in English: opción, instrucción, calificación, intimidación?

B Further study and training

Do not be put off by more complex language.

1 You may meet a task in which you have to tick **two** boxes for each question.

2 At a higher level, you need to read between the lines to judge likes, dislikes and feelings.

Escribe las letras correctas en las casillas.
Write the correct letters in the boxes.

A

Después de los exámenes de GCSE, quiero hacer un cursillo de formación profesional que se llama un GNVQ. Hay más oportunidades para hacer prácticas en una oficina o con una compañía en este tipo de cursillo. No me interesa hacer algo muy académico. Pero si quiero, podré ir a la universidad después.

B

Yo voy a pasar dos años estudiando para los exámenes de A/S y A level. Es más o menos el equivalente español del COU. Normalmente se estudian tres o cuatro asignaturas. ¡Qué bien tener que estudiar sólo las asignaturas que te interesan!

C

Tengo la intención de hacer los exámenes de A level en mi instituto. Es muy interesante estudiar una asignatura a fondo. Creo que es una buena preparación para los estudios universitarios que haré más tarde.

D

En julio, espero trabajar con mi tío que es fontanero. Hacer nueve o diez años de estudios obligatorios es suficiente, ¡y no quiero hacer más! Mi tío me va a pagar cuatro días de la semana, y voy a ir a una escuela técnica los jueves para obtener los títulos profesionales necesarios.

1 ¿Quiénes piensan ir a la universidad? ☐ ☐

2 ¿Quién va a ganar dinero? ☐

3 ¿A quiénes les gusta estudiar? ☐ ☐

4 ¿Quién está harto/a de estudiar? ☐

5 ¿Quiénes van a trabajar y estudiar al mismo tiempo? ☐ ☐

Q Can you put these verbs into the pure future: <u>voy a ir</u> ...; <u>voy a hacer</u> ...; <u>voy a estudiar</u> ...; <u>voy a trabajar</u>?

PRACTICE

Write a paragraph explaining what you want to do after your exams, and why. Use the expressions above in activity B to help.

To indicate the future, you can use <u>voy a</u> with the infinitive of the verb: <u>voy a hacer un cursillo</u> (I'm going to do a course). You can also use the future tense: <u>haré un cursillo</u>.

Vocabulary/grammar

A Work, career and future plans

Remember
The phrase <u>Si tuviera</u> ... (If I had ...) is useful here, to give you an opportunity to use the conditional tense: <u>Si tuviera más dinero, iría a la universidad.</u> (If I had more money, I would go to university.)

¿Qué planes tienes para el futuro?	What plans have you got for the future?
¿En qué te gustaría trabajar?	What kind of work would you like to do?
(No) Quiero ... preferiría ... tendré que ...	I (don't) want ... I'd prefer ... I will have to ...
ser (médico/a), tener que decidir	to be (a doctor), to have to decide
trabajar en el sector de (la industria)	to work in (industry)
tratar con (el público, los animales, los niños)	to work with (the public, animals, children)
tener un trabajo (científico, físico, artístico)	to do a (scientific, physical, artistic) job
¿En que trabajan tus padres?	What do your parents do?
Mi madre/padre es (comerciante).	My mother/father is (a shop-owner).

albañil	bricklayer	ingeniero/a	engineer
abogado/a	lawyer	jubilado/a	retired
camarero/a	waiter	mecánico	mechanic
cartero/a	post-person	médico/a	doctor
comerciante	shop-owner	peluquero/a	hairdresser
dentista	dentist	profesor/a	teacher
empleado/a de	employee of	programador/a	programmer
enfermero/a	nurse	recepcionista	receptionist
fotógrafo/a	photographer	secretario/a	secretary
granjero/a	farmer	técnico/a	technician

el comercio	business, commerce	en el extranjero	abroad
un empleo	a job	buscar, hacer	to look for, to do
una empresa	a firm, company	estudiar, viajar	to study, to travel
la enseñanza	teaching	ganar dinero	to earn money
la hostelería	hotel trade	pedir una beca	to ask for a grant
los servicios médicos	medical services	obtener un préstamo	to get a loan
el turismo	tourism	casarse	to get married

B Social issues, choices and responsibilities

¿Cuáles son ...	Which are ...
los problemas sociales más importantes	the most important social problems
de hoy en día/que te preocupan?	today which worry you?
Muy importante es ...	... is very important.
la presión del grupo partidario, el paro.	peer-group pressure, unemployment.
Tenemos que hacer más/algo diferente	We have to do more/something different
para ayudar a los que (toman drogas).	to help those who (take drugs).

utilizar, abusar	to use, to abuse	drogarse	to take drugs
tomar, dañar	to take, to harm	emborracharse	to get drunk
ser alcohólico/a	to be an alcoholic	el tabaquismo	tobacco addiction
fumar cigarillos	to smoke cigarettes	el desempleo	unemployment
la droga, alcohol	drugs, alcohol	el hambre	hunger
estar parado/a	to be unemployed	mantenerse sano/a	to stay healthy

C Impersonal verbs

These are verbs which follow the same pattern as **gustar** (page 19).
The literal meanings are given in brackets.

doler *to hurt*	Me duele la cabeza. *I've got a headache. (My head hurts me.)*
encantar *to delight*	Le encanta el fútbol. *He loves football. (Football delights him.)*
faltar *to be lacking*	Me falta un tenedor. *I haven't got a fork. (A fork is lacking to me.)*
hacer falta *to be necessary*	Me hace falta más tiempo. *I need more time. (More time is necessary to me.)*
interesar *to interest*	Me interesa mucho el golf. *I'm interested in golf. (Golf interests me.)*
quedar *to remain*	Quedan dos galletas. *There are two biscuits left. (Two biscuits remain.)*
sobrar *to be an excess of*	Sobra pan. *There's bread left over. (There is an excess of bread.)*

Note that with each, you will need to use an indirect object pronoun:
me, te, le, nos, os, les (page 19).

¿Te interesa este chico? Le duele el brazo. Os encanta la paella, ¿verdad?	*Are you interested in this lad?* *His arm hurts.* *You love paella, don't you?*

1 Put the following sentences into Spanish. Words to help are in brackets.
  a I need more money. (**hacer falta/más/dinero**)
  b There are three tickets left over. (**sobrar/tres/entradas**)
  c Are you (usted) interested in museums? (**interesar/museos**)
  d We are missing two glasses. (**faltar/dos/vasos**)
  e Her leg aches. (**doler/la pierna**)

D Adverbs

Adverbs describe verbs and actions. They are words like 'quickly', 'suddenly'.
Take the feminine form of the adjective, and add **-mente**:

ADJECTIVE	FEMININE FORM	ADD -MENTE	
entusiasmado	entusiasmada	entusiasmadamente	*enthusiastically*
triste	triste	tristemente	*sadly*

Some common adverbs have other forms:
bien (*well*), **mal** (*badly*), **despacio** (*slowly*), **rápido/rápidamente** (*quickly*).
When there are two adverbs together, the first one loses the **-mente**:
Conduce cuidadosa y lentamente. *He drives carefully and slowly.*

THE BARE BONES

➤ Getting to know about official forms, such as ID forms or a CV feature fairly frequently in the exam.

➤ You need to understand job advertisements.

A Your CV

WRITE

1 In the exam, you may be asked to show you understand a CV or you may have to write one yourself.

2 The headings on this CV will also be useful for simpler forms or ID cards.

Rellena el formulario con los detalles de abajo.
Complete the form with the details below.

CURRICULUM VITAE

1	Apellidos:	_____
2	Nombre:	_____
3	Edad:	_____
4	Fecha de nacimiento:	_____
5	Lugar de nacimiento:	_____
6	Nacionalidad:	_____
7	Estado Civil:	_____
8	D.N.I./Pasaporte:	_____
9	Dirección (+código postal):	_____
10	Teléfono:	_____
11	Estudios:	_____
12	Cargos que ha ejercido?	_____
13	Información complementaria: (p.ej. pasatiempos)	_____
14	Empleo ideal:	_____

Remember
Spanish forms ask for surnames (apellidos) because Spaniards have two names: the father's and the mother's surname.

García Morales   Médica   17 años
Fotografía/baloncesto   Carmen
                Lima, Perú.   10-4-1984
    Fotografía/baloncesto   peruana   36 741
                    802C
    Calle San Agustín, 18, 2oD, 28002, Madrid   (91) 746 65 71

soltera   Instituto San Ignacio, Madrid (BUP, COU)

        Prácticas de trabajo en el Hospital San Juan de Dios

Q Complete your own CV. Use the form on the right to guide you.

B Job advertisements

Don't worry if you can't understand every word.

1 In the next activity, you'll be reading four short job advertisements and matching each job to the most appropriate person.

2 First scan the texts which you have to match up. Can you see any similarities between any of the words in the speech bubbles and the words in the advertisements? For example, **hermanas** might be connected to **hijos**. What other connections can you find?

Para cada jóven, busca el anuncio más apropiado.
Find the most appropriate advertisement for each young person.

Remember
If you're writing about your own experience, use the preterite tense to say what kind of work you've done already: <u>pasé</u> ... <u>meses trabajando</u> (I spent ... months working), <u>trabajé como</u> ... (I worked as a ...)

Q Can you say in English when each of the people who placed these advertisements want help?

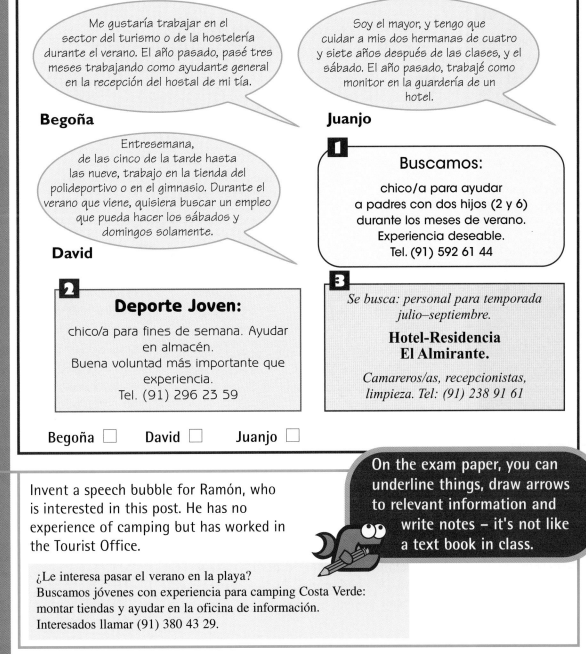

Me gustaría trabajar en el sector del turismo o de la hostelería durante el verano. El año pasado, pasé tres meses trabajando como ayudante general en la recepción del hostal de mi tía.

Begoña

Soy el mayor, y tengo que cuidar a mis dos hermanas de cuatro y siete años después de las clases, y el sábado. El año pasado, trabajé como monitor en la guardería de un hotel.

Juanjo

Entresemana, de las cinco de la tarde hasta las nueve, trabajo en la tienda del polideportivo o en el gimnasio. Durante el verano que viene, quisiera buscar un empleo que pueda hacer los sábados y domingos solamente.

David

1
Buscamos:
chico/a para ayudar a padres con dos hijos (2 y 6) durante los meses de verano. Experiencia deseeable.
Tel. (91) 592 61 44

2
Deporte Joven:
chico/a para fines de semana. Ayudar en almacén.
Buena voluntad más importante que experiencia.
Tel. (91) 296 23 59

3
Se busca: personal para temporada julio–septiembre.
Hotel-Residencia El Almirante.
Camareros/as, recepcionistas, limpieza. Tel: (91) 238 91 61

Begoña ☐   David ☐   Juanjo ☐

PRACTICE

Invent a speech bubble for Ramón, who is interested in this post. He has no experience of camping but has worked in the Tourist Office.

On the exam paper, you can underline things, draw arrows to relevant information and write notes – it's not like a text book in class.

¿Le interesa pasar el verano en la playa?
Buscamos jóvenes con experiencia para camping Costa Verde: montar tiendas y ayudar en la oficina de información.
Interesados llamar (91) 380 43 29.

Future plans

➤ Say what your plans for the future are.

➤ Write a longer letter in the exam.

A Future plans

WRITE

Remember
You can bring language from other topics in here: you might like to say what you're good at at school, to explain what you want to do in the future, e.g. Soy fuerte en ciencias y saco muy buenas notas. Por eso (for this reason), me gustaría trabajar en la investigación.

Q How many sentences can you make from the boxes A–C within five minutes?

Q Now prepare a few sentences about your own plans for the future.

1 You need to prepare a short paragraph about your hopes and plans for the future.

2 Use the language in the boxes A–C to help.

3 First, work out how to say the sentences 1–6 in Spanish.

> Escribe las frases 1–6 en español.
> Write sentences 1–6 in Spanish.

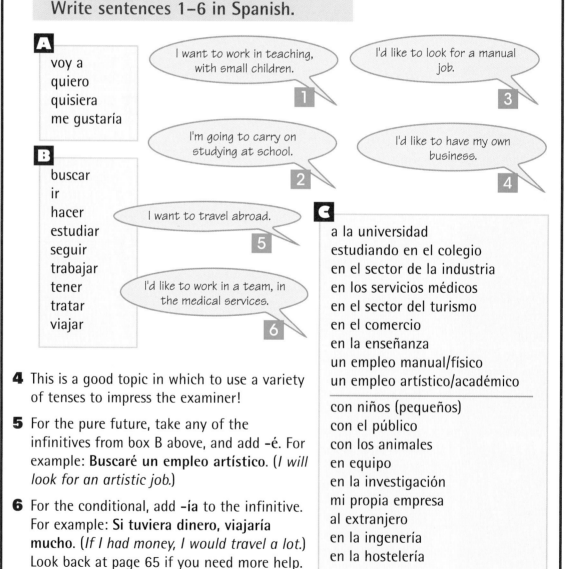

A
voy a
quiero
quisiera
me gustaría

B
buscar
ir
hacer
estudiar
seguir
trabajar
tener
tratar
viajar

1 I want to work in teaching, with small children.

2 I'm going to carry on studying at school.

3 I'd like to look for a manual job.

4 I'd like to have my own business.

5 I want to travel abroad.

6 I'd like to work in a team, in the medical services.

C
a la universidad
estudiando en el colegio
en el sector de la industria
en los servicios médicos
en el sector del turismo
en el comercio
en la enseñanza
un empleo manual/físico
un empleo artístico/académico

con niños (pequeños)
con el público
con los animales
en equipo
en la investigación
mi propia empresa
al extranjero
en la ingeniería
en la hostelería

4 This is a good topic in which to use a variety of tenses to impress the examiner!

5 For the pure future, take any of the infinitives from box B above, and add -é. For example: **Buscaré un empleo artístico.** (*I will look for an artistic job.*)

6 For the conditional, add -ía to the infinitive. For example: **Si tuviera dinero, viajaría mucho.** (*If I had money, I would travel a lot.*) Look back at page 65 if you need more help.

B Job applications

READ

1 You may be asked to read a longer passage or letter.

2 You may also have to write one (usually around 150 words) in the Higher paper.

3 It needs to include a range of tenses, descriptions and opinions.

4 Read the letter below, and do the activity.

KEY FACT

To be eligible for higher marks, use a variety of tenses.

Escoge la palabra correcta para cada espacio.
Choose the correct word for each gap.

Remember

If you're aiming at a grade C or above, you need to show how you can use a variety of tenses: a past tense, the present tense and a future tense.

a chicas

b asignaturas

c útil

d puestos

e cuatro

f niños

g bastante

h trabajar

I desorganizada

j fácil

k verano

l trabajadora

Q Look at the verbs in the letter – can you find an example of each of the following tenses: present, future, preterite, conditional?

62 Barnham Way,
Glasgow,
Escocia,
16 de marzo

Muy señor mío

Acabo de ver su anuncio de plazas vacantes para ...(1)... monitores en el camping Arenas Doradas en su página de web, y quiero solicitar uno de estos ...(2)... .

Me gustaría trabajar en España durante el ...(3)... que viene, para mejorar mis conocimientos de la lengua española. El español es una de las ocho ...(4)... que estudio para los exámenes de GCSE (equivalente al BUP en España) en junio. Lo entiendo muy bien y lo hablo ...(5)... bien. También sé hablar un poco de francés, lo que será muy ...(6)... en un camping cerca de la frontera con Francia.

El año pasado, trabajé como monitor en un hotel en el oeste de Escocia. Me gustó mucho. Me llevé muy bien con los ...(7)..., y soy muy cortés, reponsable y ...(8)... . Estaré disponible para ...(9)... a mediados de julio y puedo seguir trabajando hasta finales de septiembre.

Quedo a la espera de sus gratas noticias,
le saluda atentamente,
Janice Armstrong

PRACTICE

Write a letter in Spanish to the Hotel Espléndido, requesting the post which most appeals to you. Use Janice's letter as a model.

Hotel Espléndido, Paseo Marítimo, MALAGA: buscamos camareros/as y ayudantes generales (piscina, guardería), verano julio–septiembre.

Check over your writing in the exam. Pay attention to nouns and the endings of adjectives (masculine/feminine, and singular/plural), and verbs (correct tense and person).

Social issues and choices

THE BARE BONES

➤ You will be expected to understand information about social issues.

➤ You may have to answer questions about attitudes and feelings.

A Social issues

WRITE

Q A number of Spanish words in this topic look like English ones. Under which of the three headings would these words go: <u>inyecciones de heroína</u>, <u>el alcoholismo</u>, <u>el tabaco</u>?

1 Do not be put off by material which looks more difficult.

2 Many words and expressions will be easy to group into 'families': try the task below.

> Escribe cada expresión 1–9 en el espacio correcto.
> Write each expression 1–9 in the correct space.

el abuso del alcohol	*la droga*	el tabaquismo

1 ser alcohólico/a	4 tomar drogas	7 drogarse
2 fumar	5 los fumadores	8 los cigarrillos
3 emborracharse	6 beber demasiado	9 ser drogadicto/a

B Your concerns

KEY FACT

SPEAK

Remember
You can use just nouns, e.g., <u>la guerra</u> (war); or verb infinitives, e.g. <u>evitar</u> (to prevent, avoid).

> Keep it simple: it will be easier to remember!

1 Which social issues most concern you?

2 Use the dictionary to prepare, if necessary.

> <u>Completa estas frases.</u> Complete these sentences.

a *¿Cuáles son los problemas sociales más importantes?*
   En mi opinión, son ... (e.g. el desempleo).

b *¿Cuáles son las cosas que más te preocupan?*
   Me preocupa(n) ... (e.g. la guerra).

c *¿Qué se debe hacer para mantenerse sano/a?*
   (No) debemos ... (e.g. abusar el alcohol).

C Concerns for the future

EY FACT

Look for the overall theme in each piece of text.

READ

1 Now try the activity below.

2 You have to read each text and match them to one of the topics A–F.

Remember
The exam will
test the
vocabulary
which your exam
board expects
you to know for
each topic, so do
not omit any
sections.

Escribe cada número 1–4 en la casilla apropiada.
Write each number 1–4 in the correct box.

1
Lo que más me preocupa, es el futuro: el horror del desempleo. Mi padre, como muchos otros, pasó diez años sin ganar dinero, y yo no quiero ser como él. Mi pueblo antes era lleno de vida pero ahora está muerto. **Ángel**

2
Lo más difícil para mí, es que todos mis compañeros se emborrachan y se drogan regularmente. Hasta este momento, he resistido – ¿pero en el futuro …? **Carmelina**

Q Who has to
put up with
something? Who
says they are
worried? Who
doesn't find
something easy?

3
Mis padres esperan que yo vaya a seguir los pasos de mi abuelo y mi hermano mayor, y ser medico – pero no quiero. No me interesa. Preferiría viajar un poco, ver el mundo. No estoy bastante seguro de mí mismo para decírselo. **Íñigo**

4
Aunque yo nací aquí, y tengo un pasaporte de este país, no me trata bien la gente. Nosotros de otro color – es decir, no blanco – tenemos que aguantar la discriminación y los insultos en la calle. A veces, me hace llorar. **Zohora**

A	la guerra	D	las expectativas de la familia	
B	el racismo	E	la presión del grupo paritario	
C	el paro	F	el hambre	

EY FACT

You will need to identify attitudes and emotions.

3 Towards the end of the Higher paper in reading and listening, you may have to answer questions in English. This may not be as easy as it looks! You will need to 'read between the lines' to work out how someone is thinking and feeling.

PRACTICE

Re-read the four texts from section C above. Answer the following questions in English.

1 Why does Ángel not want to follow in his father's footsteps?
2 What is Ángel's village like now?
3 What would Íñigo prefer to do?
4 Why does Íñigo find it difficult to talk to his family?
5 How does Zohora feel about what happens to her in the street?
6 How would you describe Carmelina's attitude to the future?

Check the number of marks allocated to each question. If it says 'two marks' then you need to give two pieces of information.

THE BARE BONES
➤ Simple listening tasks with picture symbols.
➤ You will need to answer questions in English.

The listening section contains a variety of exam-type activities, based on the Bitesize Revision TV programmes which you can video. Check the Bitesize website for when they should be shown.

A School subjects

KEY FACT

You may not need to put a tick in every box.

LISTEN

1 Listen to the section '¿Qué asignaturas estudias?'

2 Put a tick in the correct column every time you hear that subject mentioned.

Escucha y escribe ✔✔ en las casillas correctas.
Listen and put ✔✔ in the correct boxes.

Remember
When talking about English (language) use lenguaje: estudio lenguaje y literatura means 'I study (English) language and literature'.

1 1066 1492 1918 1945	2 el mundo	3 ¡hola! ¡hola! ¡hola! ¡hola!	4 GB GB	5	6 23 +14 37	7	8

B Likes and dislikes

KEY FACT

Do not expect to hear on tape exactly what is written on the page: listen for meaning.

LISTEN

1 You may be asked to decide in which order information is given on the tape.

2 The section begins '¿Qué asignatura prefieres?'

Escucha las cuatro (4) jóvenes. ¿En qué orden hablan?
Escribe cada número 1–4 en la casilla correcta.
Listen to the four young people. In which order do they speak? Write each number 1–4 in the correct box.

Me gusta el inglés porque ...

A	es divertido		D	no es dificil	
B	la asignatura me gusta		E	el profesor es simpatico	
C	no tengo muchos deberes				

Q How many ways do you know of expressing likes and preferences? E.g. Me gusta ...

C Daily routine

EY FACT

LISTEN

If the questions are in English, you must answer in English.

1 The first section of the exam may have **questions in English**.

2 **Read each question** carefully, so you know **what to listen for**.

3 Listen to the section 'La vuelta al colegio', as far as the word **inglés**.

Answer the following questions in English.

The new school year is beginning.

1 What is the date?

_____

2 Who is Patricia looking for?

_____

3 What does the tutor do first?

_____

4 What time does the Social Science class start on Mondays?

_____

5 Which subject do they have before English?

_____

Remember

If you are asked to write answers in English and you write a Spanish word (e.g. geografía instead of geography), you will get no mark for it.

PRACTICE

Find the clip about Noyer and Susana's day: 'La Rutina.' Listen as far as 'Los jueves tenemos un trabajo muy especial'.

Answer these questions in English.

1 How old is Susana?

_____

2 What time does Susana wake up?

_____

3 What does Susana do at half-past eight?

_____

4 Where does Susana have lunch?

_____

5 What does Noyer do after lunch?

_____

6 After her homework, what does Susana do?

_____

Listen carefully if there are two voices on the tape. Make sure you answer questions about the correct person.

Listening (2)

THE BARE BONES ➤ Further tasks with symbols.

A *House and home*

There may be extra language or information which you do not need.

1 You may have to select more than one symbol for each person.

2 Listen to the clip '¿Dónde vives?', where Yimer shows us around his house. Choose two symbols for each room. Other pieces of furniture may be mentioned: just focus on the items suggested by the symbols, and on the rooms mentioned.

Escribe las letras a–h en las casillas correctas. **Sobran dos**. Write the letters a–h in the correct boxes. There are two which are not needed.

Remember
La cocina can mean several things, depending on context: a kitchen, a cooker/stove, and cookery.

Q How does Yimer describe his house? How many rooms does it have? What size is the living room?

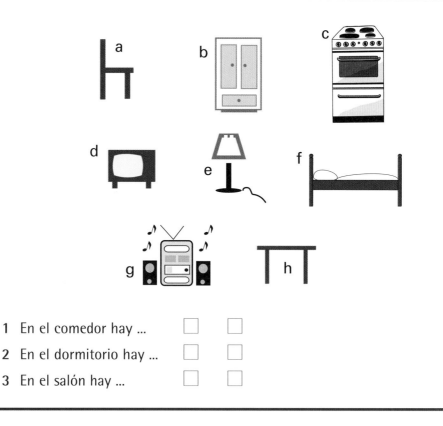

1 En el comedor hay ...   ☐ ☐

2 En el dormitorio hay ... ☐ ☐

3 En el salón hay ...   ☐ ☐

B Restaurants

EY FACT

LISTEN

Remember
Read the question carefully. Here you are asked to note the dish which no-one (nadie) asks for.

Only tick one box. If you make a mistake, make sure the examiner understands which is your final answer.

1 A common exam task is a multiple choice question with pictures.

2 You will be asked to tick one box in each row.

Escribe ✔ en las casillas correctas. Put a ✔ in the correct boxes.

1 De primero, nadie quiere ...

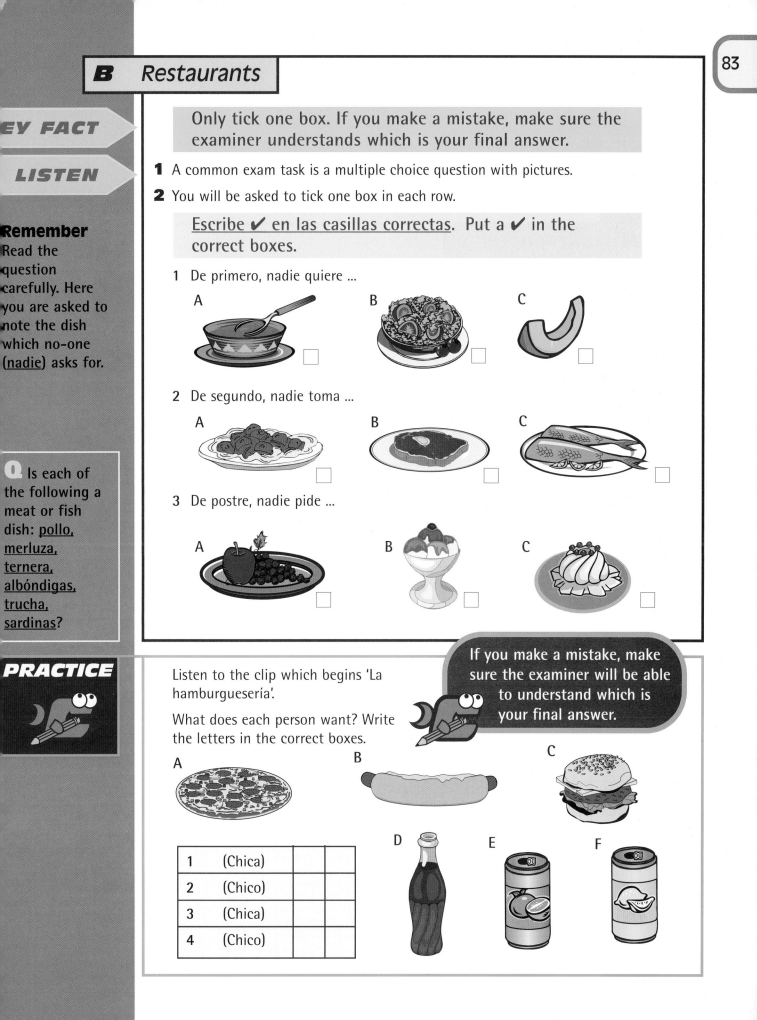

A ☐ B ☐ C ☐

2 De segundo, nadie toma ...

A ☐ B ☐ C ☐

3 De postre, nadie pide ...

A ☐ B ☐ C ☐

Q Is each of the following a meat or fish dish: <u>pollo</u>, <u>merluza</u>, <u>ternera</u>, <u>albóndigas</u>, <u>trucha</u>, <u>sardinas</u>?

PRACTICE

Listen to the clip which begins 'La hamburguesería'.

What does each person want? Write the letters in the correct boxes.

If you make a mistake, make sure the examiner will be able to understand which is your final answer.

A   B   C

D   E   F

1	(Chica)		
2	(Chico)		
3	(Chica)		
4	(Chico)		

Listening (3)

THE BARE BONES
➤ You will need to answer questions in Spanish.
➤ You will need to listen for numbers and dates.

A Introductions

KEY FACT

If you're asked to reply in Spanish, do not write any English words.

LISTEN

1 You may be asked to give brief answers in Spanish.

2 Find the clip which begins 'Hoy estamos en casa de Diana...'.

Remember
If your spelling mistake means that the word you wrote actually means something else in Spanish, you will not get a mark. Take care with words for family members, e.g. madre/padre (mother/father).

Completa la ficha en español.
Complete the form in Spanish.

1 Nombre: Diana

2 Apellido: Fernanda Llánez

3 Edad: 12 años

4 Número de personas en casa:

5 Número de hermanos:

6 Número de hermanas:

7 Animales (tipo):

B Numbers and dates

LISTEN

1 You may also have to write numbers and dates.

2 Find the clip where the reporters from Colombia introduce themselves: 'Somos el equipo de reporteros ...'.

Escribe los detalles en las casillas correctas.
Write the details in the correct boxes.

	Edad	Cumpleaños
Carolina		
Eduar		
Sarita		
Yimer		

Q How would you say the following in Spanish: 2, 12, 22, 204, 14, 40, 400?

C Personal information

LISTEN

1 Although this is a listening exam, you may have to read some Spanish.

2 Learn words like **muy** (*very*), **bastante** (*quite*), **un poco** (*a little*). They can completely alter the meaning of what is said.

3 In the preparation task below, find the pairs of sentences which have a very similar meaning.

EY FACT

Watch for negatives, like <u>no</u>: they also change the meaning of the sentence.

<u>Busca las parejas. Sobran dos frases.</u>
Look for the pairs. There are two sentences left over.

Ejemplo: 1 + 6.

1 Es un poco gordito/a.

2 Tiene el pelo corto.

3 Tiene el pelo negro.

4 Tiene le pelo rubio.

5 No es muy alto/a.

6 No es delgado/a.

7 No tiene el pelo largo.

8 Es muy gorda.

9 Tiene el pelo moreno.

10 Es bastante baja.

Q How would you say you were: quite tall, very slim, your hair was very long?

PRACTICE

Listen to the same clip as in Activity B above.

Write the initial letter of the correct person in the appropriate box.

C (Carolina), E (Eduar), S (Sarita), Y (Yimer)

¿Quién ...		
1	... tiene el pelo negro?	
2	... es delgado/a?	
3	... tiene el pelo corto?	
4	... no es muy delgado/a?	
5	... no es alto/a?	

You may hear vocabulary you do not know. In this task, you will hear the word <u>cabello</u> (means the same as <u>pelo</u>) and <u>café</u> (<u>marrón</u>). Focus on the questions you are asked: you may not need to understand everything you hear.

Listening (4)

THE BARE BONES
➤ Draw conclusions and make inferences.
➤ Choose the correct possibilities.

A Sports

LISTEN

1 As well as listening for detail, you will be expected to draw conclusions from what people say.

2 Listen to the clip which begins '¡Hola! ¿Qué deportes te gustan?', and ends 'el ciclismo'.

3 Put a tick every time you hear a sport in each of the places A–E.

Q What type of sport or hobby would you associate with these places: la discoteca, la pista de hielo, la biblioteca, el gimnasio?

> Escribe ✔✔ en las casillas apropiadas.
> Put ✔✔ in the appropriate boxes.

A la piscina					D el campo de fútbol			
B la pista de tenis					E el club de artes marciales			
C el río								

B Free time

LISTEN

1 You may meet the following type of task: you have to decide whether a statement is true, false, or whether it is not possible to say from the information given.

2 Listen to the clip which begins '¿Qué deportes practicas?' .

Remember
Check the instructions used by your particular exam board. Some may use verdadero (true), falso (false), or no se sabe (don't know).

Remember
Do not expect to hear on tape exactly the same words as are in the exam question.

> Escribe V (verdad), M (mentira), o ND (no dice).
> Write V (true), M (false), or ND (doesn't say).

Ejemplo:

1 Le gusta patinar.	V
2 Pratica dos o tres deportes.	
3 Le gusta nadar.	
4 Es miembro de un equipo de fútbol.	
5 No le interesan los artes mariales.	
6 Le gustan muchos deportes.	
7 Los deportes acuáticos no le interesan.	

C Arranging to go out

Remember
If the instruction does not tell you how many statements to tick, the number of marks allocated will give you a clue: there is usually one mark per tick.

Q What is the English for the following: <u>los fines de semana, entresemana, la semana que viene?</u>

Read the statements carefully.

1 A variation on the true/false task asks you to **tick only the phrases which are true.**

2 Pay particular attention to details like:

- **times** (quarter to, half past, etc.)
- **times of day** (this evening, tomorrow night, etc.)
- **meeting places** (inside, outside, in front of, etc.)

3 Listen to the clip where Manuel telephones Enma.

<u>Escribe ✔ al lado de las tres (3) afirmaciones verdaderas.</u>
Put a ✔ beside the three statements which are true.

1 Manuel quiere salir a bailar.	
2 Enma no quiere ir a la discoteca.	
3 Se reúnen a las ocho de la tarde.	
4 Se reúnen dentro de la discoteca.	
5 Manuel suele salir los sábados y domingos.	
6 A Manuel le gusta comer las fresas.	

PRACTICE

Find the clip in which Vanesa and Ramón buy tickets. Write V (true), M (false), or NS (doesn't say).

1 Vanesa compra tres entradas.	
2 A Vanesa le gustó mucho la película.	
3 Ramón quiere ir a la cama.	
4 Vanesa está cansada.	
5 Ramón no quiere encontrarse con Vanesa mañana.	

Read each statement carefully before listening: it might be true for one of the people on the tape, but not for the other.

Listening (5)

A Home town

LISTEN

Remember
You need to understand both big numbers and fractions. Population is expressed in thousands (mil) or millions (millones); common fractions are un cuarto (a quarter) and la mitad (half).

1 There are a variety of gap-fill activities which you may meet in the exam.

2 Find the first part of the clip about Mexico City, and do the activity.

> **Escoge el número correcto para cada espacio.**
> Choose the correct number for each gap.

a Hoy en día, hay más de _____ millones de habitantes.

b En el año dos mil, habrá unos _____ (millones).

c México está situada a _____ metros de altura.

d Un _____ de la población del país vive en la capital.

e Casi la _____ de la industria está aquí.

2000
$\frac{1}{4}$
30
900
19
$\frac{1}{2}$

B Likes and dislikes

KEY FACT

LISTEN

Remember
Small errors of spelling or grammar are not penalised.

> Keep your answer simple, and close to the original.

1 You may be asked to write something in Spanish, as well as tick a box.

2 Find the clip which begins '¿Qué prefieres – la ciudad o el pueblo?'

3 **¿Dónde quieren vivir y por qué? Escribe ✔ y la razón.**
Where do they want to live and why? Put a ✔ and the reason.

	Pueblo	Ciudad	Campo	Razón
1				
2				
3				

c   Your region

A knowledge of grammar will help you in this type of task.

1 Another type of gap-fill activity requires you to **choose words from a list**.

2 There will be a number of **extra words** which **you will not need**.

3 Use the following clues to help with the first three gaps:

- After the noun **un pueblo**, you will probably need an adjective.
- After **dos**, you will need a plural noun.
- After **se puede** you will need a verb in the infinitive form.
- Listen to the clip about Zujaira, as far as 'Es increíble'.

Remember
You may hear a word on the tape which is also on the list: this does not necessarily mean it will fit in one of the gaps.

Q What other places do the young people mention? There are several (varios) of them.

<u>Escoge la palabra correcta para cada espacio.</u>
Choose the correct word for each gap.

4 Find the clip which begins 'Qué prefieres – la ciudad o el pueblo?'

> Zujaira es un pueblo ☐, con dos mil habitantes. Hay casas de dos ☐, y un edificio donde se puede ☐ deporte. En el pueblo, hay ☐: una panadería, una farmacia y una tienda de ☐. Para los jóvenes, lo más importante es que hay un lugar donde se puede ☐.

1 bailar	5 ropa	8 discoteca
2 tiendas	6 apartamentos	9 hacer
3 grande	7 pisos	10 pequeño
4 jugar		

PRACTICE

Listen to the clip about Zujaira, beginning with the section 'Con las aceitunas hacemos un excelente aceite de oliva'. Does each person have a positive or negative view of the village? Why? Put a ✔ and write the reason in Spanish.

You may not hear the words 'positive' or 'negative'. You may have to deduce from what they say whether each person feels positive or negative.

	Positivo	Negativo	Razón
Juanjo			
Nerea			
Clara			

Listening (6)

THE BARE BONES
➤ Follow maps and routes.
➤ Multiple choice questions.

A Directions

LISTEN

1 If you are asked to follow directions on a map, use these hints to help:
- Make abbreviated notes first time you listen.
- Check your notes against the map to work out the route.
- On the second listening, trace your directions to check you have the right route.
- Now listen to the clip where Ana organises a treasure hunt.

KEY FACT

> Study the maps before you listen.

Remember
Make sure you know your right (<u>derecha</u>) from your left (<u>izquierda</u>) before you start!

> <u>Escucha las indicaciones y escoge la letra correcta.</u>
> Listen to the directions and choose the correct letter.

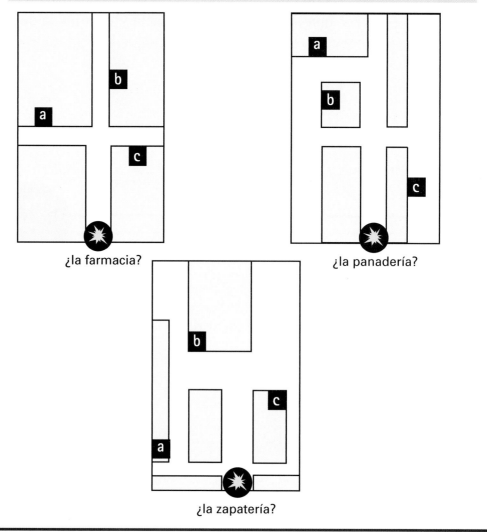

¿la farmacia?

¿la panadería?

¿la zapatería?

Q How would you direct someone to each of the places marked a, b, and c on the maps?

B Shopping

Concentrate on one section at a time.

1 You may have to cope with a **multiple choice question**.

2 Do not be put off by a lot of text.

3 **Read** the options **carefully**. Try and **discard the unlikely ones first**.

4 Look for **options which are very similar**. Put a dot or question mark beside them to remind yourself to listen with extra care.

Find the clip which begins 'Vanesa, Israel, Sara y Ramón están aquí de compras'.

Escribe ✔ en las casillas apropiadas.
Put a ✔ in the appropriate boxes.

1 Vanesa busca:

☐ **a** una camisa mediana

☐ **b** una camiseta pequeña

☐ **c** una camisa grande

2 Israel quiere:

☐ **a** una cazadora mediana

☐ **b** una cazadora pequeña

☐ **c** una camisa pequeña

3 Ramón quiere:

☐ **a** unos pantalones beige

☐ **b** unos pantalones marrones

☐ **c** unos pantalones grises

4 Ramón necesita la talla:

☐ **a** 21

☐ **b** 31

☐ **c** 30

5 Hay también chaquetas en:

☐ **a** negro y naranja

☐ **b** blanco y marrón

☐ **c** naranja y blanco

6 Sara va a probarse:

☐ **a** la naranja

☐ **b** la blanca

☐ **c** la roja

Remember

f you change your mind after ticking box, and want to ick a different ne, make sure ou score out your irst attempt. f the examiner ees two ticks, you vill get no marks, even if one of hem is correct!

Q What does Vanesa ask if she can do? What does the shop assistant think about the garment?

PRACTICE

Listen to the initial section again of the same clip, and answer these questions in English.

1 What does Laura think about fashion?

_____

2 Which season of the year is mentioned?

_____

3 For which occasion are the clothes being considered?

_____

4 What are the four young people going to do?

_____

5 What does Israel think of the jacket?

_____

If you are not sure of an answer, make an educated guess rather than leave a blank. For example, in question 3 you have a one-in-four chance of getting it right!

Listening

There are many different task types in the exam. You will meet some more of them in the other sections. Here are examples of further test types, with some for you to try yourself on the opposite page.

A   Gap-fill tasks

Scan the sentences and the words in the list before the tape starts.
Try and narrow down the kind of word which will be needed in each gap.

For example:

- Before **años** there will probably be a number.
- After **hay que** you need a verb in the infinitive.
- After **ser** will be a noun or an adjective.
- After **un** you need a masculine noun.
- After the adjective **buen** you'll need a noun.

Example 1
Find the clip where Virginia talks about her plans for the future.

Escribe la letra correcta en cada casilla.

1 Hay exámenes importantes a la edad de $\boxed{g}$ años.

2 Si quieres ir a la universidad, hay que $\boxed{c}$ los exámenes.

3 Virigina quiere ser $\boxed{e}$.

4 Tiene que hacer un $\boxed{h}$ de tres años en la universidad.

5 Todos sus amigas quieren conseguir un buen $\boxed{a}$ después.

a	trabajo	c	aprobar	e	profesora	g	dieciocho
b	poder	d	dieciséis	f	ísica	h	curso

> **Tip**
> Don't expect to hear on tape the same words as are on the list. For example, what other word do you know for job/work, apart from **trabajo**?

B   Matching information you hear to written summaries

As you will know by now, there is more than one way of expressing something!

This type of task tests your ability to do this. You may see and hear related words: like **médico/medicina**.

Example 2
Find the section where Maite asks '¿Dónde vas a ir para seguir tus estudios?'

Escucha los cuatro jóvenes: ¿qué quieren hacer?
Escribe cada número 1–4 en la casilla correcta.

A Pienso estudiar medicina.	4	D Quisiera ser guardia un día.	3
B Espero pasar dos años en Argelia.		E Voy a pasar dos o tres meses en Cuba.	
C Quiero trabajar en el periodismo.	1	F Espero enseñar más tarde.	2

> **Tip**
> Take care with numbers, places, people: we do hear Argelia and Cuba mentioned, but the number of months or years does not match.

Question 1

Find the clip where Virginia asks 'Y tú, ¿qué quieres hacer en el futuro?'

Escucha los cinco jóvenes: ¿qué sueños tiene para en el futuro?
Escribe cada número 1–5 en la casilla correcta.

A	Quiero grabar un disco un día.	
B	Quiero hacer un trabajo físico.	
C	Voy a tener una escuela de idiomas.	
D	Espero ser jefa de un partido político.	
E	Escribiré un libro sobre la historia de la Guerra Civil.	
F	Me gustaría ser dueño de un periódico.	

Question 2

Listen to the clip where Antonio talks about Salamanca.

Escribe el número correcto en cada casilla.

Antonio tiene ☐ años y vive en Salamanca, donde el ☐ se llama el Tormes.

El puente es muy ☐, pero todavía sirve. Hay edificios antiguos y ☐.

La ciudad tiene muchas ☐. Muy ☐ también es la Plaza Mayor.

1 nueve	3 antiguo	5 río	7 grande	9 romano
2 iglesias	4 quince	6 célebre	8 catedrales	10 nuevos

Question 3

Find the clip which begins 'Granada es una capital andaluza'.

Escribe ✔ *al lado de las tres (3) frases verdaderas.*

1	La capital es andaluza.	
2	Los romanos y los árabes quedaron poco tiempo.	
3	La ciudad tiene influencia árabe.	
4	Los castillos fueron construidos por los romanos.	
5	Isabel y Fernando eran reyes cristianos.	

Reading

A   Reading tasks with pictures

This is one of the simpler task types in the exam. You need to choose the sentence which matches each picture best. Be careful of 'false friends': words in Spanish which look like English ones, but mean something different.

> **Tip**
> There may be words which are 'false friends' to try and catch you out! False friends remind you of a word that's similar in English but means something different.

Example 1

¿De qué actividad habla cada jóven?

Escribe las letras correctas en las casillas.

A Cuando llueve, juego al ping-pong con mi hermana.   6

B Si hace buen tiempo, me gusta andar en bici.   2

C Me encanta nadar en el mar, si hace bastante calor.   4

D A veces, vamos de excursión en autocar a la sierra.   1

> **Tip**
> Underline the words which have a connection with transport.

> **Tip**
> **Autocar** is a false friend. It actually means 'bus'.

B   Drawing conclusions

This type of task is more challenging. You have to decide what the writers think or feel.
The text may not give the information directly – you will have to read between the lines.
Be careful with negatives. Do not assume that this means the writer feels negative!

Example 2

¿Qué opinan de su barrio?

¿Cada persona es positiva (P), negativa (N) o indiferente (I)?

Escribe ✔ en la casilla correcta.

Tip
Don't assume
that there will
have to be a
tick in each
column. One
might have
none!

1   Las calles están sucias, hay ventanas rotas, papeles por
todas partes y no hay ningún sitio donde pueden jugar
los niños.

2   No paso mucho tiempo en mi barrio, y no me doy
cuenta de como es. Tengo una novia en las afueras, y
suelo ir allí los fines de semana. Me da igual.

3   Aunque las calles están estrechas y la gente no tiene
mucho dinero, mi barrio está muy animada. Todo el
mundo es simpático y no hay ni violencia ni jaleo.

	P	N	I
1		✔	
2			✔
3	✔		

Tip

Make sure you understand what to do. In a
similar task type you might be asked to say
whether a viewpoint is **positivo o negativo**
(positive or negative). Here, **indiferente** means
doesn't particularly care one way or the other.

Some questions for you to try

Question 1

¿Qué les gusta hacer en su tiempo libre?

Escribe las letras correctas en las casillas.

1	En mi tiempo libre me gusta mucho leer.	
2	Me encantan las películas de aventura.	
3	Cuando puedo, voy de paseo en el campo.	
4	¿Lo que más me gusta? ¡Tomar el sol en la playa!	

a
b
c
d
e
f

Question 2
¿Qué opinan de sus vacaciones?

Escribe P (positivo), N (negativo) or P+N.

1 El hotel era muy cómodo, y muy cerca de la playa. Lo peor era el ruido: había una discoteca cerca, donde bailaban hasta las tres de la madrugada.

2 ¡Hacer camping cuando llueve todos los días no es agradable! Ropa mojada, agua en los cereales, frío por la noche – ¡no ha sido la mejor experiencia de mi vida!

3 Pasamos una en un barco de vela, con seis otras personas que no conocimos antes. ¡Ahora, sí! Hicimos viajes bonitos por la costa, pero no había mucho sitio.

	P	N	P+N
1			
2			
3			

Question 3
¿Qué tiempo hará en cada región?

Escribe la letra correcta para cada frase.

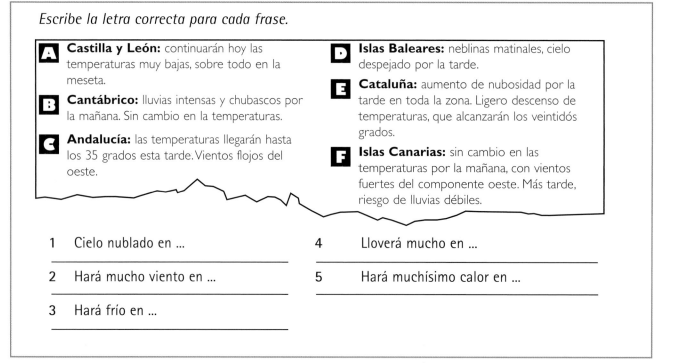

A Castilla y León: continuarán hoy las temperaturas muy bajas, sobre todo en la meseta.

B Cantábrico: lluvias intensas y chubascos por la mañana. Sin cambio en la temperaturas.

C Andalucía: las temperaturas llegarán hasta los 35 grados esta tarde. Vientos flojos del oeste.

D Islas Baleares: neblinas matinales, cielo despejado por la tarde.

E Cataluña: aumento de nubosidad por la tarde en toda la zona. Ligero descenso de temperaturas, que alcanzarán los veintidós grados.

F Islas Canarias: sin cambio en las temperaturas por la mañana, con vientos fuertes del componente oeste. Más tarde, riesgo de lluvias débiles.

1 Cielo nublado en …

2 Hará mucho viento en …

3 Hará frío en …

4 Lloverá mucho en …

5 Hará muchísimo calor en …

Speaking

A Role-plays

- You will almost certainly be expected to do more role-plays in the exam.
- Your part of the role-play will tell you in English what to say.
- Some role-plays may give you more choice of what to say (as on the opposite page).
- Some, like the example opposite, require you to stick closely to what is given.
- You may be in a formal situation (shopping, buying tickets): use **usted** for 'you'.
- You may be talking to a Spanish friend: use the familiar **tú**.

Tip
Remember that you do not need to put words like 'tell', 'explain' or 'say' into Spanish – just imagine that someone is whispering these instructions in your ear.

B   Higher role-plays

These are more unstructured, and you will need to use a variety of tenses: past, present and future. The scene will be set in English for you, and the details given in Spanish. Read the sample question and the notes 1–4 which follow it.

TEACHER'S/EXAMINER'S ROLE	YOUR CARD (MODEL ANSWER IN BRACKETS)
Buenos días.	*Say you want a return ticket to Madrid.* (Quiero un billete de ida y vuelta a Madrid.)
Muy bien.	*Ask how much it is.* (¿Cuánto es?)
Quince euros.	*Ask what platform it leaves from.* (¿De qué andén sale?)
El número dos.	*Ask where you can buy a magazine.* (¿Dónde puedo comprar una revista?)
Hay un quiosco allí.	*Say thank you.* (Gracias.)

Tip
To say how long you have been doing something, use the present tense with **desde hace**: **aprendo ... desde hace cuatro años.** (I've been learning ... for four years).

Tip
An exclamation mark means you have to respond to the teacher's/ examiner's question.

Example

It's the last day of your Spanish holiday when you badly cut your finger. You also feel sick. You go to the doctor. When you see this ! you will have to respond to something which you have not prepared. Your teacher will play the part of the doctor and will speak first.

TEACHER'S/EXAMINER'S ROLE	YOUR CARD
Buenas tardes. ¿Qué le pasa?	• (1) Tu problema y cuándo ocurrió.
¿Cómo ocurrió esto?	• (2) Tu explicación – qué hacías y cómo ocurrió.
¿Qué comió al mediodía?	• (3) Qué comiste al mediodía, y dónde.
La enfermera va a ponerle una venda, y hay que volver a verme mañana.	• (4) !

1 You usually have to explain what has happened. Here, you also need to say when. You will need a preterite tense: **Esta mañana, me he cortado el dedo. Tengo náuseas también.** *(This morning I cut my finger. I feel sick too.)*

2 You have to explain what you were doing. This often needs an imperfect tense or an imperfect continuous tense: **Estaba preparando un plato para la cena, y cortando los tomates.** *(I was preparing a dish for dinner and cutting the tomatoes.)* Use the preterite to explain the event itself: **Cogí el cuchillo** *(I picked up the knife)*, **no sé lo que pasó exactamente.** *(I don't know what happened exactly.)*

3 You need to explain where you ate, and what you ate. Use the preterite tense: **Comí una hamburguesa que compré en un quiosco en el parque.** *(I ate a hamburger that I bought at the kiosk in the park.)*

4 You can do some preparation by thinking about the situation: the instructions say it is the last day of your holidays – might you be asked to come back tomorrow? Think of a reason why you can't, and use a future tense, for example: **Voy a volver a Gran Bretaña mañana. Tendré que estar en el aeropuerto a las nueve.**

Some questions for you to try

Role-play 1 (Foundation level)

TEACHER'S/EXAMINER'S ROLE	YOUR CARD
Buenos días, ¿qué desea? Aquí tiene. Siga todo recto. Está a la derecha. A las ocho. ¿Usted es de Gran Bretaña?	*Say you'd like a brochure about the town. Ask how to get to the swimming-pool. Ask what time it closes. Explain that you're here on holiday.*

Tip
If you can't remember the exact word, try something which gets across the same idea. If you can't remember the word for brochure, you could say **información**.

Role-play 2 (Foundation level)

YOUR CARD	TEACHER'S/EXAMINER'S ROLE
Explain to your friend that you're thirsty. Say what you want to drink. Say two things you'd like to eat. Ask if s/he would like to go to the cinema later.	¿Qué quieres? ¿Quieres comer algo? Vale, ya voy. Sí, con mucho gusto.

Tip
You're talking to a friend here, so use **tú** for you.

Role-play 3 (Higher level)

It's the last day of your Spanish exchange, and you realise that you have lost your bag in the sports centre. You go to reception. Your teacher will play the part of the receptionist and will begin.

TEACHER'S/EXAMINER'S ROLE	YOUR CARD
Buenas tardes. ¿Cuándo ocurrió esto? ¿Cómo era? – ¿ Qué contenía? ¡Usted habla bien español! ¿Desde hace cuánto tiempo lo aprendes?	(1) Tu problema. Lugar de la pérdida. (2) Explica lo qué hacías y cómo ocurrió. (3) Descripción. Artículos que contenía (4 detalles). (4) !

Tip
Check the instructions carefully: are you asked to give a certain number of details? Make sure you do!

Writing

A   Replying to questions

- You may be asked a number of questions in Spanish to which you have to reply.
- You need to write a sentence for each, and you can choose how to answer. You will probably need to write about 30 words.

Tip
There are a number of marks for accuracy: the fewer mistakes you make in spelling and grammar, the more you will gain.

Example 1

¡Hola!

¿Qué tal? Yo, fatal. ¡Tengo mucho trabajo, y quiero salir al centro!

Francisco.

You have just received this email from your Spanish friend Francisco. He wants to know about the subjects you like and your school routine, what you do after school, what you're going to do on Saturday, and if you have a job.

1 ¿Qué asignaturas te gustan?

Me encantan la historia y los trabajos manuales.

2 ¿Cómo es tu profesor/a de español?

Es divertida pero estricta.

3 ¿Qué haces en la hora de comer?

Tomo un bocadillo y un zumo de fruta en la cantina.

4 ¿Qué haces por la tarde?

Hago mis deberes y veo la tele.

5 ¿Qué vas a hacer el sábado?

Voy al cine con mis amigos.

6 ¿Tienes algún empleo?

En las vacaciones, trabajo en un supermercado.

Tip
You will need to write around 90 words.

B   Writing a letter

The letter may be formal (e.g. to a hotel or Tourist Office) or informal, to a friend.

Example 2

> You have just received a letter from a friend, who wants to know about what you did at Christmas, what it was like for you, how your studies are going, and your plans for the year. Here are some suggestions you could include in your reply.
>
> **Menciona:**
> - qué hiciste el día de Navidad:
>   *Me levanté temprano para abrir los regalos, y fui a la casa de mis abuelos para comer.*
>
> - qué comiste/bebiste:
>   *Comimos pavo con verduras y patatas, y pasteles y dulces de postre.*
>
> - cómo pasaste el resto de las vacaciones:
>   *Viajé en tren a Madrid para ir de compras en los grandes almacenes.*
>
> - qué vas a hacer este año:
>   *Voy a ir al gimnasio y a la piscina para mantenerme en forma.*
>
> - cómo van tus estudios:
>   *Saco buenas notas en los idiomas, pero creo que voy a suspender en matemáticas.*
>
> - tu instituto – tu opinión:
>   *Mi instituto es grande, pero bastante antiguo. Los profesores son simpáticos, y creo que la disciplina es buena.*
>
> **Pregunta:**
> - algo sobre la rutina de Marcos.
>   *¿Cuántas horas de clases tienes tú al día?*

Tip
Check the instructions carefully. There may be a set number of tasks to do (e.g. 8), and one of them may require you to ask a question.

Some questions for you to try

Question 1

> You are shopping for presents to take home from Spain.
> Write the Spanish for four presents you might buy.

turrón
un plato de cerámica
_____
_____
_____
_____

Tip
Although small spelling errors will not be penalised, you will not get a mark for a word which is not recognisable or which might be a different Spanish word: e.g. **plato** (plate), **plata** (silver).

Question 2

You've just received this letter from a Spanish friend. Write back to him.
He wants to know about your village or town, what young people can do, the weather,
getting to school, learning Spanish and your best friend.

> ¡Hola! Me preguntas sobre mi pueblo - no es grande, pero se puede ir a la discoteca
> los viernes. Voy con mis amigos. Aquí, hace calor - ¿y allí?

- ¿Cómo es tu pueblo o ciudad?
- ¿Qué pueden hacer los jóvenes?
- ¿Qué tiempo hace allí en este momento?
- ¿Cómo vas al instituto?
- ¿Qué opinas de aprender el español?
- ¿Cómo es tu mejor amigo/a?

Tip
You can use 'en mi opinión',
'creo que', 'me parece que'
to indicate your opinion.

Question 3

You have just returned from a visit to Spain at Easter, and receive a letter from a friend there.
She wants to know about your journey home, your impressions of your stay, relationships at
home and school life, and plans for the summer.

Menciona:
- tu viaje de vuelta.
- qué es lo que más te gustó de España.
- algo que no te gustó mucho.
- tus relaciones con los miembros de tu familia.
- los problemas de los jóvenes donde vives tú.
- cómo se puede mejorar tu instituto.
- tus planes para el verano.

Tip
Check that you refer to past, present and
future events, using a range of tenses,
and that you have included your
opinion(s) or feelings.

Pregunta:
- algo sobre su tiempo libre.

Topic checker

- After you've revised a topic, go through these questions.
- Put a tick if you know the answer, a cross if you don't (you can check your answers by looking back at the page reference).
- Try the questions again until you've got a column that is all ticks! Then you'll know you can be confident!

Section A My world

Personal information (pp.8, 12)

Can you say what your name is? (p.8)	☐	☐	☐
Can you spell your surname? (p.8)	☐	☐	☐
Can you say the Spanish alphabet? (p.8)	☐	☐	☐
Can you say what age you are? (p.8)	☐	☐	☐
Can you explain when your birthday is? (p.8)	☐	☐	☐
Can you say what nationality you are? (p.8)	☐	☐	☐
Can you name eight different nationalities? (p.8)	☐	☐	☐
Can you give the feminine form of adjectives of nationality which end in -o, -és, -án? (p.8)	☐	☐	☐
Can you ask someone else questions about their name, age, birthday and nationality? (p.8)	☐	☐	☐

Family and friends (pp.8, 13)

Can you explain how many people there are in your family? (p.8)	☐	☐	☐
Can you say who they are? (p.8)	☐	☐	☐
Can you explain that you're an only son/daughter? (p.8)	☐	☐	☐
Can you describe someone's relationship status? (e.g. married, divorced)? (p.8)	☐	☐	☐
Can you talk about your wider family (e.g. uncle, grandmother)? (p.8)	☐	☐	☐

Interests and hobbies (pp.9, 14, 15)

Can you say what sports you play? (p.9)	☐	☐	☐
Can you explain what other things you do in your free time? (p.9)	☐	☐	☐
Can you say whether you play a musical instrument or not? (p.9)	☐	☐	☐
Can you talk about why you like, or don't like, particular sports or hobbies? (pp.9, 14, 15)	☐	☐	☐
Can you ask others about sports or hobbies they do? (pp.9, 14, 15)	☐	☐	☐
Can you explain when you have free time? (p.15)	☐	☐	☐

Your home and town/village (pp.9, 16–18, 20)

Can you say what type of house or flat you live in? (p.9)	☐	☐	☐
Can you say what number of rooms it has? (p.9)	☐	☐	☐
Can you describe your bedroom and what is in it? (pp.9, 17)	☐	☐	☐
Can you say where you live, and where that is? (p.18)	☐	☐	☐
Can you give your address? (p.18)	☐	☐	☐
Can you describe your town or village? (pp.18, 20)	☐	☐	☐

Daily routine, school subjects, likes and dislikes (pp.18, 22–4)

Can you say how many subjects you study, and what they are? (p.18)	☐	☐	☐
Can you explain which subjects you like, and why? (pp.18, 24)	☐	☐	☐
Can you name the subjects you don't like, and give a reason? (pp.18, 24)	☐	☐	☐
Can you describe your school, and say what facilities it has? (p.18)	☐	☐	☐
Can you describe your routine on a school day? (p.22)	☐	☐	☐
Can you explain when you have meals? (p.23)	☐	☐	☐
Can you say what you like to eat and drink? (p.23)	☐	☐	☐

Section B   Holiday time and travel

Asking the way (pp.26, 30)

Can you ask how to get to different places? (p.26)	☐	☐	☐
Can you ask if there's a (chemist's) near here? (p.26)	☐	☐	☐
Can you give directions? (p.26)	☐	☐	☐
Can you explain exactly where a place is? (p.26)	☐	☐	☐
Can you name types of streets and public buildings? (p.26)	☐	☐	☐
Can you name twelve different shops? (p.26)	☐	☐	☐
Can you understand simple notices in shops? (p.30)	☐	☐	☐

Travel and transport (pp.26, 30, 32)

Can you buy different types of train and bus tickets? (p.26)	☐	☐	☐
Can you say and ask when trains or buses arrive and depart? (p.27)	☐	☐	☐
Can you request other details: platform, changes, length of journey? (p.27)	☐	☐	☐
Can you ask about cost and supplements? (p.27)	☐	☐	☐
Can you name six different means of transport? (p.27)	☐	☐	☐
Can you name places within a station (e.g. waiting room)? (p.27)	☐	☐	☐

Tourism and weather (pp.27, 34)

Can you ask what the weather's like? (p.27)	☐	☐	☐
Can you ask what the forecast is? (pp.27, 34)	☐	☐	☐
Can you describe the main types of weather? (p.27)	☐	☐	☐
Can you say what the weather will be like? (p.27)	☐	☐	☐
Can you ask for items in the Tourist Office? (p.27)	☐	☐	☐
Can you describe what there is to do in an area? (p.27)	☐	☐	☐

Accommodation and holidays (pp.36, 38, 40)

Can you reserve different types of rooms? (p.36)	☐	☐	☐
Can you say for how many people and nights? (p.36)	☐	☐	☐
Can you ask about mealtimes? (p.36)	☐	☐	☐
Can you ask about facilities (e.g. lifts, parking)? (p.38)	☐	☐	☐
Can you explain that something is missing or not working? (p.36)	☐	☐	☐
Can you ask if there's room for a tent? (p.36)	☐	☐	☐
Can you describe where you go on holiday, and what you usually do? (p.40)	☐	☐	☐
Can you describe a past holiday: where you went, what you did? (p.40)	☐	☐	☐

Restaurants (pp.36, 41)

Can you explain what you would like for each course? (p.36)	☐	☐	☐
Can you order for a friend? (p.36)	☐	☐	☐
Can you ask what there is for vegetarians? (p.36)	☐	☐	☐
Can you ask what a dish contains? (p.36)	☐	☐	☐
Can you find out if you can pay by credit card? (p.36)	☐	☐	☐
Can you complain that something is dirty or missing? (p.36)	☐	☐	☐
Can you check if the service charge is included? (p.36)	☐	☐	☐

Services and problems (pp.36, 42, 43)

Can you name the parts of the body? (p.42)	☐	☐	☐
Can you explain you don't feel well, and what's the matter? (p.36)	☐	☐	☐
Can you say how long you've been feeling ill? (p.36)	☐	☐	☐
Can you explain that you've lost something and describe it? (p.43)	☐	☐	☐

Section C Work and lifestyle

Household chores, healthy living (pp.44, 48, 49)

Can you explain how you help out at home? (p.44)	☐	☐	☐
Can you say what you like or hate doing and why? (p.44)	☐	☐	☐
Can you describe what others do, or don't do, to help? (p.44)	☐	☐	☐
Can you explain how to stay healthy? (p.44)	☐	☐	☐
Can you describe what is good and bad for health? (p.44)	☐	☐	☐
Can you say what your diet is like? (p.44)	☐	☐	☐
Can you say what we should/shouldn't eat? (p.44)	☐	☐	☐
Can you give five expressions in Spanish associated with drinking and tobacco? (pp.44, 48)	☐	☐	☐

Leisure and going out (pp.45, 50, 51)

Can you ask what's on TV or at the cinema? (pp.45, 51)	☐	☐	☐
Can you name six different types of film or programmes? (pp.45, 51)	☐	☐	☐
Can you name other types or places of entertainment? (p.45)	☐	☐	☐
Can you ask how much tickets cost? (p.45)	☐	☐	☐
Can you find out where your seats are? (p.45)	☐	☐	☐

Shopping (pp.45, 52, 53)

Can you ask where you can buy an item? (p.45)	☐	☐	☐
Can you say what you'd like, ask if they have ...? (p.45)	☐	☐	☐
Can you explain that's all, thank you? (p.45)	☐	☐	☐
Can you say you have no change, or you only have a ☐10 note? (p.45)	☐	☐	☐
Can you say what size you take in clothes and shoes? (p.45)	☐	☐	☐
Can you describe what you like to wear? (p.52)	☐	☐	☐
Can you name ten items of clothing? (p.45)	☐	☐	☐
Can you give the Spanish for six containers or quantities? (pp.45, 53)	☐	☐	☐

Contacting others (pp.54, 56)

Can you answer the phone and ask to speak to someone? (p.54)	☐	☐	☐
Can you ask who is speaking? (p.54)	☐	☐	☐
Can you explain that the line is engaged or not answering? (p.54)	☐	☐	☐
Can you ask for the code and number? (p.54)	☐	☐	☐
Can you ask if you can leave a message? (p.54)	☐	☐	☐
Can you give the Spanish for a phonebook, a mobile phone and email? (p.54)	☐	☐	☐
Can you express your annoyance or disappointment? (p.56)	☐	☐	☐

Part-time jobs (pp.54, 58)

Can you say if you have a job and what you do? (p.54)	☐	☐	☐
Can you describe when you work, how many hours, and when you start and finish? (pp.54, 58)	☐	☐	☐
Can you say how much you earn? (p.54)	☐	☐	☐
Can you give your opinion of your job? (p.54)	☐	☐	☐
Can you ask others about their jobs, hours, earnings and opinions? (p.54)	☐	☐	☐

Work experience (pp.54, 60, 61)

Can you explain where you did your work experience? (p.54)	☐	☐	☐
Can you describe how long it lasted? (p.54)	☐	☐	☐
Can you say how you travelled to your workplace, and how long it took? (p.54)	☐	☐	☐
Can you give details of the hours you did? (p.54)	☐	☐	☐
Can you describe the work you had to do? (p.54)	☐	☐	☐
Can you say what you thought of your experience? (p.60)	☐	☐	☐
Can you say what you're going to do next year? (p.61)	☐	☐	☐
Can you say what you plan to do? (p.61)	☐	☐	☐
Can you explain what you usually do? (p.61)	☐	☐	☐

Section D The young person in society

Character and relationships (pp.62, 66, 67)

Can you ask what someone's character is like? (p.62)	☐	☐	☐
Can you describe your own personality? (p.62)	☐	☐	☐
Can you name eight positive personality characteristics? (p.62)	☐	☐	☐
Can you name eight negative personality characteristics? (p.62)	☐	☐	☐
Can you say what you think a good friend should be like? (p.62)	☐	☐	☐
Can you say how well you get on with different members of your family? (p.62)	☐	☐	☐
Can you name six words for moods or feelings? (pp.62, 67)	☐	☐	☐
Can you describe how someone else behaves? (p.66)	☐	☐	☐
Can you say that your friend makes you angry? (p.62)	☐	☐	☐
Can you explain that relationships are good? (p.62)	☐	☐	☐
Can you give the Spanish for 'usually, normally'? (p.62)	☐	☐	☐
Can you remember the Spanish for 'sometimes'? (p.62)	☐	☐	☐

The environment (pp.63, 68, 69)

Can you say what we should do to protect the environment? (p.63)	☐	☐	☐
Can you express what we should not do? (p.63)	☐	☐	☐
Can you name six items which we should save, recycle or cut down on? (p.68)	☐	☐	☐
Can you give the Spanish for six verbs which show what we do to the environment (e.g. to consume – **consumir**)? (p.63)	☐	☐	☐
Can you describe the negative effects of what we do (e.g. it's harmful)? (p.63)	☐	☐	☐
Can you say what you're worried about, environmentally? (p.63)	☐	☐	☐
Can you give six Spanish words connected with traffic and fuel? (p.63)	☐	☐	☐
Can you say in Spanish 'oilslick', 'flood', 'ozone layer'? (p.63)	☐	☐	☐
Can you explain there should be more or less of something? (p.63)	☐	☐	☐

Education and social issues (pp.63, 70–2, 78)

Can you say what you want to do next year? (pp.63, 71)	☐	☐	☐
Can you say where you hope to go? (pp.63, 71)	☐	☐	☐
Can you give your opinion on school rules? (pp.63, 71)	☐	☐	☐
Can you say what you think of school uniform? (pp.63, 71)	☐	☐	☐
Can you explain what you think of discipline in your school? (pp.63, 71)	☐	☐	☐
Can you describe the advantages of going to school? (pp.63, 71)	☐	☐	☐
Can you say what you think the greatest social problems are? (p.72)	☐	☐	☐
Can you explain who, in your opinion, we need to help? (p.78)	☐	☐	☐

Work and careers (pp.63, 71, 72, 74–7)

Can you explain what jobs your parent(s) do(es)? (p.72)	☐	☐	☐
Can you name eight different jobs or careers? (p.72)	☐	☐	☐
Can you say which kind of work you would like to do? (p.72)	☐	☐	☐
Can you give a reason for your choice? (p.72)	☐	☐	☐
Can you say that you don't want to decide yet? (p.72)	☐	☐	☐
Can you explain that you will have to get a loan or a grant? (p.72)	☐	☐	☐
Can you ask someone else about his/her future plans? (p.72)	☐	☐	☐
Can you say you want to go to university? (p.63)	☐	☐	☐
Can you explain you'd like to do a GNVP? (p.71)	☐	☐	☐
Can you say you hope to get married one day? (p.72)	☐	☐	☐
Can you explain you'd like to work in business or industry? (p.72)	☐	☐	☐
Can you give two Spanish words for 'unemployment'? (p.72)	☐	☐	☐

A, some (p.10)
Fill in the gaps.

	masculine	feminine
(s)	**un** hermano *a brother*	__ hermana *a sister*
(pl)	__ hombres *some men*	__ mujeres *some women*

The (p.10)
Fill in the gaps.

	masculine	feminine
(s)	**el** tío *the uncle*	__ tía *the aunt*
(pl)	__ chicos *the boys*	__ chicas *the girls*

Plural nouns (p.10)
Make the nouns plural.

un libro	30	*libros* ....
una mesa	15	....
un tablón	4	....
un ordenador	3	....
una luz	8	....
un estante	2	....
un póster	5	....

Adjectives (p.10)
Write the feminine adjective.

masculine	feminine
italiano	**italiana**
catalán	
escocés	
español	
marrón	
rosa	

The present tense (p.11)
Complete the verb endings.

	hablar *(to speak)*	comer *(to eat)*	vivir *(to live)*
yo	habl**o**	com__	viv__
tú	habl__	comes	viv__
él, ella, usted	habl__	come	vive
nosotros	hablamos	com__	vivimos
vosotros	habláis	coméis	viv__
ellos, ellas, ustedes	habl__	comen	viven

Irregular present tense verbs (p.11)

a Write in the 'yo' form of each verb.

dar (to give)	doy	saber (to know how to)	
conocer (to know a person)		salir (to go out, leave)	
hacer (to do, make)		traer (to bring)	
poner (to put, set, lay)		ver (to see)	

Irregular present tense verbs (p.11)

a Write in the 'yo' form of each verb.

IR	(to go)	voy			va		vais	
TENER	(to have)		tienes			tenemos		tienen
ESTAR	(to be)			está			estáis	
SER	(to be)	soy				somos		

b Fill in the blanks.

There are two verbs to be: **ser, estar**.

Use [   ] to indicate position, and temporary moods.

Use [   ] for describing people, places, things.

c Complete the missing parts of the verbs.

The immediate future (p.19)

Fill in the blanks.

To say what you're going to do:

Use the verb [   ],

followed by [a], and the

[   ] of another verb.

Gustar (p.19)

Fill in the gaps.

Me gust<u>a</u> el dibujo.
No me gust_ la historia.
Me gust_ _ las matemáticas.
No me gust_ _ los deberes.

Indirect object pronouns (p.19)
Fill in the gaps.

I like	__me__	gusta/n
you like	__	gusta/n
he/she/you likes	__	gusta/n
we like	__	gusta/n
you like	__os__	gusta/n
they/you like	__	gusta/n

Reflexive verbs (p.19)
Fill in the missing reflexive pronouns:

yo	____ lavo
tú	____ lavas
él, ella, usted	____ lava
nosotros	__nos__ lavamos
vosotros	__os__ laváis
ellos, ellas, ustedes	____ lavan

Question words (p.28)
Write in the Spanish.

where?	*¿dónde?*
how much?	_____
how?	_____
what?	_____
when?	_____
who?	_____
why?	_____

A/de (p.28)
Fill in the blanks.

a The Spanish for *to* is **a**.

When followed by **el** it becomes ☐.

b The Spanish for *of* or *from* is **de**.

When followed by **el** it becomes ☐.

Positive commands (p.29)
Fill in the missing endings or parts.

	TÚ	USTED
-ar	habla	habl_
-er	com_	com_
-ir	escrib_	escrib_

	TÚ	USTED
(cruzar)	cruza	
(torcer)		tuerza
(coger)	coge	
(seguir)		siga

The perfect tense (p.29)
Complete the endings and missing words.

	YO	
-ar (dejar)	he	dej _ _ _
-er (comer)	he	com _ _ _
-ir (salir)	he	sal _ _ _

he	**escrito**	*I've written*
		I've done
		I've put on, set
		I've broken
		I've seen

The regular preterite tense (p.37)

Complete the verb endings.

	hablar	comer	vivir
yo	habl__	comí	viv__
tú	habl__	com__	viviste
él, ella, usted	habl__	comió	viv__
nosotros	hablamos	com__	vivimos
vosotros	hablasteis	com__	vivisteis
ellos, ellas, ustedes	habl__	comieron	viv__

Irregular preterite verbs (p.37)

Fill in the missing parts of the verbs.

SER, IR	to be, to go	fui		fue		fuisteis	
DAR	to give		diste		dimos		dieron

The pretérito grave (p.37)

Complete the endings.

INFINITIVE		STEM
to be	estar	estuv-
to do, make	hacer	
to be able to	poder	
to put, set	poner	
to want to	querer	
to have	tener	
to come	venir	

yo	-e
tú	-____
él, ella, usted	-o
nosotros	-____
vosotros	-isteis
ellos, ellas, ustedes	-____

Direct object pronouns (p.46)

a Fill in the missing pronouns.

SINGULAR	
me	me
_____	you (informal)
_____, le	it, him
_____	it, her
le (m), la (f)	you (formal)

PLURAL	
_____	us
os	you (informal)
_____ (m), las (f)	them (objects)
les (m), _____ (f)	them (people)
les (m), las (f)	you (formal)

b Fill in the blanks.

Direct object pronouns usually come

the verb:

E.g. ¿El pantalón? Lo compro.

They can be added on to the

of an infinitive:

E.g. ¿La camisa? Sí, quiero comprarla.

Demonstrative adjectives (p.46)

Fill in the missing words.

	(ms)	(fs)
this	este	_____
that	_____	esa
that (there)	aquel	_____

	(mpl)	(fpl)
these	_____	estas
those	esos	_____
those (there)	_____	aquellas

Demonstrative pronouns (p.46)

Fill in the gap.

(this/that one, these/those ones)
are the same as the adjectives
above, but have an [   ]
on the first 'e':

Verbs of obligation (p.47)

Complete with the correct verbs.

(have to, must)	_____
(ought to, should)	_____
(one has to)	_____

Se ... (p.47)

Complete the boxes

Se	+	_____ (part of the verb)	=	One ... They ... People ... We ...

(comer)	(beber)	(escribir)
Se come	Se _____	Se _____

The regular imperfect tense (p.55)

Complete the endings.

	-AR	-ER	-IR
yo	hablaba	beb____	vivía
tú	habl____	bebías	viv____
él, ella, usted	hablaba	beb____	vivía
nosotros	habl____	bebíamos	viv____
vosotros	hablábais	beb____	vivíais
ellos, ellas, ustedes	habl____	bebían	viv____

Irregular imperfect tense verbs (p.55)

Fill in the missing parts.

IR	(to go)	iba	_____	_____	íbamos	_____	_____
SER	(to be)	_____	eras	_____	_____	érais	_____
VER	(to see)	veía	_____	veía	_____	veíais	_____

The gerund and continuous tenses (p.55)

Complete the gaps.

	Remove	Add	Example		
-ar verbs	-ar		andar	⟶	
-er verbs		-iendo	comer	⟶	
-ir verbs			escribir	⟶	

Present continuous: use the present tense of the verb [   ] + gerund.

Imperfect continuous: use the [   ] tense of the verb estar + gerund.

The future and conditional tenses (p.64)

Fill in the blanks and complete the verb endings.

1 The future tense indicates what [   ] happen.

2 The conditional indicates what [   ] happen.

3 The endings are the same for [**-ar**] [   ] and [   ] verbs.

	FUTURE	CONDITIONAL
yo	hablaré	hablar__
tú	hablar___	hablarías
él, ella, usted	hablará	hablar___
nosotros	hablar___	hablaríamos
vosotros	hablaréis	hablar___
ellos, ellas, ustedes	hablar___	hablarían

Irregular future/conditional stems (p.64)

Complete the verbs.

	INFINITIVE	STEM
to do, make	hacer	har-_____
to be able to	poder	_____
to put, set	poner	_____
to want to	querer	_____
to have	tener	_____
to come	venir	_____

Ser/estar (p.65)

Complete the grid.

SER
1 Permanent characteristics
2
3 Time

ESTAR
1
2 Feelings, moods
3

Negative commands (p.65)

Fill in the missing endings.

	TÚ	USTED
-ar	no hables	no habl__
-er	no com__	no com__
-ir	no escrib__	no escrib__

	VOSOTROS	USTEDES
-ar	no habléis	no habl__
-er	no com__	no com__
-ir	no escrib__	no escrib__

Impersonal verbs (p.73)

Complete correctly.

to hurt	doler
to delight	
to be lacking	
to be necessary	
to interest	
to remain, be left over	
to be an excess of	

Me _duele_ la espalda.

Te _____ el deporte, ¿no?

Le _____ un cuchillo.

Nos _____ más dinero.

Os _____ mucho el tenis, creo.

_____ tres manzanas.

_____ vino.

Adverbs (p.73)

Fill in the boxes and complete the grids.

To form adverbs, take the masculine form of the [   ].

Now make it [   ] and add -mente.

rápido	➜	. . . .	+	-mente	➜	. . . .
lento	➜	. . . .	–	-mente	➜	. . . .
fácil	➜	. . . .		-mente	➜	. . . .

well	
badly	
slowly	

There are two words for 'quickly':

[   ]

[   ]

Check your grammar in the exam.

- Gender of nouns: do I need **el**, ..., **los** or ... ? Should it be ..., **una**, **unos**, ...?
- The word for *to/at* is **a**; followed by **el**, it becomes ... .
- The word for *of/from* is **de**: followed by **el**, it becomes ... .
- Endings on adjectives: masculine, ... , singular, ...?
- Endings on verbs: is this the correct .... (preterite/present/future, etc.)?
- Impersonal verbs like **gustar** need an indirect object pronoun: should it be **me**, ..., **le**, ..., **os**, ...?
- Direct object pronouns: use ... and **les** for people, and **lo**, **la**, ..., **las** for things.

Answers

Pages 10–11

B Plural nouns: cuatro dormitorios, dos terrazas, dos balcones, tres pasillos, dos garajes, cuatro televisores

C Adjectives: baja, mayor, alta, delgada, verdes, marrón, cortés, callada, impaciente, habladora, menores, inteligentes, graciosos

F Verbs: 1 conoces, eres 2 vivo, haces 3 estamos, tiene 4 es, vais 5 sé, salimos

Page 13

C Family and friends: 1-C, 2-G, 3-A, 4-F, 5-E, 6-D

Q When's your birthday? How many people are there in your family?

Page 14

A Sports and hobbies: 1-e, 2-c, 3-a, 4-h, 5-g, 6-d, 7-f, 8-b

B Likes and dislikes: Felipe - Me gusta practicar el piragüismo, y me encanta hacer footing, pero odio/no me gusta nada jugar al golf. **Raúl** - Me gusta jugar al hockey, y me encanta jugar al voleibol pero odio/no me gusta nada practicar la equitación.

Page 15

D Saying when and how often: 1 en verano, en otoño, en invierno 2 en septiembre 3 una vez por mes 4 tres veces por semana 5 los lunes por la noche 6 los martes, los sábados 7 el dieciséis de junio

Practice: 1 en invierno 2 en julio y agosto 3 dos veces por semana 4 después de las clases 5 los viernes por la noche 6 los domingos

Page 16–17

A Your home: 1 antigua 2 pequeña 3 amueblada 4 grande 5 espacioso 6 bonita 7 verde 8 nuevo

B Adding detail: 1-e, 2-i, 3-h, 4-g, 5-c, 6-d, 7-a, 8-b, 9-f

C Your bedroom: 1 cama 2 guardarropa 3 alfombra 4 estante 5 puerta 6 mesilla 7 cómoda 8 armario

Complete the gaps: 1 compartir 2 bastante 3 azul 4 noche 5 estante 6 deberes 7 pósters

Page 21

C Understanding descriptions: 1-M, 2-V, 3-ND, 4-M, 5-V, 6-M, 7-M, 8-ND, 9-V

Page 22

A Daily routine: 1 A qué hora 3 Cómo 5 Cuánto 7 Cuántas 9 Cuándo 11 Dónde 13 Cuántas 15 A qué hora

Page 23

B Mealtimes: Dani-M, Alicia-D, Nuria-T, Paco-M, Lorenzo-D

Practice: Nombre – Ben; Comida preferida – la tortilla española; Detesta – el coliflor; Le gusta beber – zumo de fruta; Vegetariano/a – sí

Page 24

A Likes and dislikes: Correct sentences are 2, 3, 4, 5, 7

Page 25

B After the exams: 1 ¡Voy a descansar un rato! 2 Me gustaría buscar un empleo y ganar dinero. 3 Voy a volver al instituto y seguir estudiando. 4 Espero hacer el COU.

Page 28

B A/De: 1-c, 2-f, 3-g, 4-h, 5-b, 6-a, 7-d, 8-e

Page 29

D Perfect tense: 1 Has visitado 2 Has perdido 3 he probado 4 ha salido 5 ha dejado

Page 30

A In the street: 1-F, 2-A, 3-H, 4-B, 5-I, 6-G, 7-C, 8-D

Page 31

B Buying tickets: 1 un billete sencillo/de ida sólo para Madrid 2 un billete no fumador 3 un billete de primera clase 4 un billete de ida y vuelta para Calahorra 5 dos billetes sencillos/de ida sólo para Sevilla 6 un bonobús

Role-play: 1 Quisiera un billete de ida y vuelta para Toledo, por favor. 2 ¿A qué hora llega el tren a Toledo? 3 ¿De qué andén sale? 4 ¿Hay que cambiar/hacer transbordo?

Practice: 1-D, 2-C, 3-A, 4-B, 5-E, 6 (distracter) 7-F

Page 32

A **Asking where a place is:** 1 Sí, hay uno en la Avenida de Cádiz. 2 Sí hay una en la Avenida de Cádiz. 3 Sí, hay una en la Calle Goya. 4 Sí, hay unos/servicios en la Calle Sol. 5 Sí, hay uno en la Plaza Mayor. 6 Sí, hay una en la Plaza Mayor. 7 Sí, hay unas en la Avenida de Cádiz.

A5: 1 por 2 uno 3 enfrente 4 entre 5 gracias 6 nada

Q 1 ¿Dónde está el estanco? 2 ¿Dónde está la cafetería? 3 ¿Dónde está la farmacia? 4 ¿Dónde están los servicios? 5 No veo el mercado, ¿Dónde está? 6 ¿Dónde está la parada de autobuses? 7 ¿Dónde están las tiendas turísticas en esta parte de la ciudad?

Page 33

B **Directions:** 1 baje la calle 2 tuerza a la izquierda 3 tome la primera a la izquierda 4 siga todo recto 5 al final de la calle 6 cruce la plaza 7 tuerza a la derecha 8 toma la segunda a la derecha 9 siga hasta el cruce 10 hasta los semáforos

B3: 1 la catedral 2 el mercado 3 la parada de autobuses 4 los servicios 5 el banco 6 la Oficina de Turismo

Practice: 1 Siga todo recto hasta el cruce con la del Paseo San Juan. Está allí enfrente de la cafetería. 2 Siga todo recto hasta el final de la calle. Tuerza a la derecha, y está allí, enfrente. 3 Hay una farmacia en la Calle Goya. Siga todo recto y está a la izquierda entre el Corte Inglés y el banco. 4 Siga todo recto hasta el semáforo. Está allí a la izquierda.

Page 34

A **Talking about the weather:** En el norte está nublado y llueve. En el sur hace sol y calor. En las montañas hay tormenta y nieva. En la costa hay niebla y hace frío.

B **Forecasts:** lluvia b, f, h ; calor e, g, j; nubes d, i; frío a, c

Page 35

C **Town and region:** 1-g, 2-a, 3-f, 4-h, 5-d, 6-b, 7-e, 8-c

Practice: 1-V, 2-M, 3-M, 4-ND, 5-V, 6-ND

Page 38

A **Enquiring about facilities:** 1 Hotel 2 piscina 3 playa 4 habitación 5 teléfono 6 televisión 7 doce 8 perros

B **Booking in:** 1 ¿El Hotel Córdoba? 2 ¿Puedo reservar una habitación doble? 3 Para seis noches, desde el siete de agosto hasta el trece. 4 ¿Se admiten perros? 5 ¿La habitación tiene teléfono? 6 Quisiera una habitación con vista al mar 7 ¿Hay una piscina? 8 Perfecto, gracias.

Page 39

C **Campsites:** (in this order) A, L, I, B, H, J, F

Page 40

A **On holiday:** 1 padres 2 bonito 3 lejos 4 buena 5 mal 6 nunca 7 natación

B **Using different tenses:** 1 Paso mis vacaciones en Escocia. 2 El pueblo es bonito y turístico. 3 Visito castillas, y voy de paseo por la playa y la costa. 4 Hace bastante calor, pero llueve a veces. 5 Ayer, alquilé una bici. 6 El fin de semana voy a ir de excursión en barco.

Page 41

C **Restaurants:** ticks for 2, 3, 4, 6, 7

C2: De primero, quiero ensalada de tomates. Me gustaría probar la tortilla española con patatas fritas. Para mí, un helado de fresa. Quisiera un agua mineral con gas.

Q ¿Hay algo para vegetarianos? ¿Qué recomienda? ¿Qué es ... exactamente? ¿El servicio está incluido?

Page 42

A **Parts of the body:** 1 la cabeza 2 la nariz 3 los oídos 4 la boca 5 la muela 6 la garganta 7 los ojos 8 la espalda 9 el brazo 10 la mano 11 el dedo 12 el estómago 13 la pierna 14 el pie

Q 1 Me duele la cabeza. 2 Me duele la nariz. 3 Me duelen los oídos. 4 Me duele la boca. 5 Me duele la muela. 6 Me duele la garganta. 7 Me duelen los ojos. 8 Me duele la espalda. 9 Me duele el brazo.

10 Me duele la mano. 11 Me duele el dedo.
12 Me duele el estómago. 13 Me duele la pierna.
14 me duele el pie.

B **Explaining what's the matter:** no estoy muy bien,
no me siento bien; la cabeza, el estómago; desde
anoche; nóuseas, fiebre

Q Tengo la fiebre del heno. Tengo una insolación.

Page 43

C **Lost property:** ticks for 1, 3, 4, 7

Practice: 1 Apellido(s): Josef 2 Nombre: Martine
3 Domicilio: Limoges 4 Nacionalidad: francesa
5 Fechas de estancia en España: 15-22 julio
6 Artículo: bolsa 7 Color/material: negro, cuero
8 Lugar: servicios, estación de ferrocarril
9 Contenido: monedero, pasaporte, llaves
10 Valor total: 35 euros

Page 46

A **Direct object pronouns: a** este **b** esa
c aquel **d** ésa **e** ésos **f** aquellas

Page 47

C **Verbs of obligation: a** Debo recoger mi
dormitorio./I ought to tidy my room. **b** Todos
tenemos que ayudar en casa./We all have to help
at home. **c** Hay que aprender el vocabulario, si
quieres aprobar el examen./You have to learn
vocabulary if you want to pass the exam.
d Los jóvenes deben hacer más ejercicio
físico./Young people ought to take more physical
exercise. **e** Felipe, tienes que coger las entradas
para el cine./Felipe, you have to get the cinema
tickets. **f** Anita y Paco, hay que recoger el salón./
Anita y Paco, you have to tidy up the living-room.

D **Se:** se bebe, se comen, se toma, se fuman, se
toman, se fabrica

Page 48

A **Staying healthy:** ticks for A, B, C, F, H

B **Reading for detail: a** Alicia **b** Paco **c** Alicia
d Joaquín **e** Joaquín **f** Paco

C **Chores:** 1 recoger mi habitación/cuarto/ dormitorio
2 poner la mesa 3 pasar la aspiradora 4 preparar
la cena 5 hacer las compras 6 ayudar

Page 50

A **Invitations** (Javi and Marifé): 1 el 2 de
3 por 4 el 5 por 6 por

Page 51

B **TV and film:** Miguel-N, Alicia-P+N, Santi-P,
Belén-N, Pablo-N, Teresa-P+N, Eduardo-N

Page 52

A **Clothes:** 1-b, 2-c, 3-c, 4-c, 5-b, 6-b

Page 53

Practice: un kilo de plátanos, una lata de tomates,
una botella de limonada, uvas, siete, cincuenta

Page 55

D **Imperfect tense:** iba, estaba, tomaba,
empezábamos, tenían, gustaba, achivaba, hacía,
cogía, repartía, solíamos

Page 56

A **Phone messages:** 1-e, 2-h, 3-f, 4-d, 5-a, 6-b, 7-g,
8-c

A3: ¿Hablo con la secretaria? Me pone con el
señor Gómez, por favor. ¡Qué pena!/fastidio/lata!
¿Me puede llamar a las cuatro y media? Soy Sam
Thompson, de Gales. Mi número de teléfono es el
740692. El prefijo es 01745. Gracias, adiós.

Page 57

B **Means of travel:** 1-f, 2-e, 3-c, 4-a, 5-g, 6-d

C **Getting to school:** Vengo en tren. Vivo bastante
lejos del instituto. Es rápido y cómodo, pero caro.
Tardo unos veinte minutos.

Page 58

A **Part-time jobs:** 1-c, 2-f, 3-a, 4-h, 5-d, 6-e, 7-g

B **Expanding your replies:** 1 sábados 2 siete
3 nueve 4 cuatro 5 siete euros 6 interesante

Page 59

C **How you spend your money:** 1 Sabrina 2 Isabel
3 Isabel 4 Enrique 5 Sabrina 6 Sabrina

Page 60

A **Work experience:** 1-e, 2-c, 3-g, 4-a, 5-f, 6-d,
7-h, 8-b

B **Giving details: a** Trabajé en una agencia de viajes. **b** Duraron diez días. **c** Iba en autobús y andando. **d** Tardaba casi una hora. **e** Trabajaba desde las nueve hasta las cinco y media. **f** Había tres descansos de veinte minutos. **g** Era de una a dos. **h** Sí. En general, era muy divertido pero a veces era un poco repetitivo.

Page 61

Practice: 1 En una oficina de información y turismo. **2** aburrido. **3** Preparar folletos turísticos en el ordenador. **4** Seguir estudiando. **5** Gana bastante. **6** Un país sudamericano/Bolivia.

Page 64

A **Future and conditional tenses:** tendrá, aprenderá, habrá, será, iría, podría, querría, haría, habría

Page 65

B **Relative pronouns: a** que **b** quién **c** lo que **d** que **e** lo que

Page 66

A **Character:** 1–5, 2–9, 3–18, 4–12, 6–15, 7–13, 8–20, 10–16, 11–19, 14–17

B **Getting on with others – or not!:** No me llevo bien con ella. Me fastidia/irrita, y me enfado con ella. A veces hay disputas pero en general las relaciones son buenas. Un/a amigo/a bueno/a debe ser ...

Page 67

C **Moods and feelings:** deprimido/a=N, triste=N, ilusionado/a=P, estresado/a=N, enfadado/a=N, contento/a=P, preocupado/a=N, furioso/a=N, cansado/a=N, harto/a=N

C3: 1–D, 2–C, 3–B

Page 68

Q No deberíamos utilizar tantos recursos naturales, por ejemplo como el gasoleo, la electricidad y el carbon.

Page 69

B **Transport issues:** Leonora - tráfico/circulación; Adriano - caro; Paco - aparcar

Q el aparcamiento, la circulación

Page 71

B **Further study and training:** 1-AC, 2-D, 3-BC, 4-D, 5-AD

Q iré, haré, estudiaré, trabajaré

Page 73

C **Impersonal verbs: a** Me hace falta más dinero. **b** Sobran tres entradas. **c** Le interesan los museos? **d** Nos faltan dos vasos. **e** Le duele la pierna.

Page 74

A **Your CV: 1** García Morales **2** Carmen **3** 17 años, **4** 10.4.1984 **5** Lima, Perú **6** Peruana **7** Soltera **8** 36 741 802C **9** Calle San Agustín 18 20D, 280002, Madrid **10** (91) 746 65 71 **11** Instituto San Ignacio, Madrid (BUP, COU) **12** Prácticas de trabajo en el Hospital Juan de Dios **13** Fotografía/balconcesto **14** Médica

Page 75

B **Job advertisements:** Begoña 3, David 2, Juanjo 1

Page 76

A **Future plans: 1** Quiero trabajar en la enseñanza con niños pequeños. **2** Voy a seguir estudiando en el colegio. **3** Quisiera buscar un empleo manual. **4** Me gustaría tener mi propia empresa. **5** Quiero viajar en el extranjero. **6** Quisiera trabajar en un equipo, en los servicios médicos.

Page 77

B **Job applications:** 1-e, 2-d, 3-k, 4-b, 5-g, 6-c, 7-f, 8-l, 9-h

Page 78

A **Social issues:** el abuso del alcohol -1, 3, 6; la droga - 4, 7, 9; el tabaquismo - 2, 5, 8

Q las inyecciones de heroína – la droga, el alcoholismo – el abuso del alcohol, el tabaco – el tabaquismo

Page 79

C **Concerns for the future:** B-4, C-1, D-3, E-2

Q Zohora puts up with something; Ángel is worried; Carmelina doesn't find something easy.

Practice: 1 Ángel does not want to spend ten years

without any money/income, as his father had to.
2 The village is dead. 3 He'd like to travel/see the
world. 4 He doesn't feel confident. 5 It makes her
cry. 6 Carmelina feels unsure/uncertain (of her
ability to resist the pressure from her friends).

Page 80

A **School subjects:** Columns: 1 (history) = one tick;
3 (Spanish/language) = two ticks; 4 (English) = one
tick; 6 (maths) = four ticks; 7 (biology) = one tick.
No-one mentioned geography, computer studies or
sport.

B **Likes and dislikes:** A-4, B-2, D-3, E-1

Page 81

C **Daily routine:** 1 18th September 2 New teacher
3 Register the class 4 9.30 5 maths

Practice: 1 - 14; 2 - 7.30; 3 - eat breakast;
4 - dining room; 5 - plays football with his
friends; 6 - reads for a bit

Page 82

A **House and home:** 1 comedor - a+h; 2 dormitorio -
e+b; 3 salón - d+g

Q **His house is big and old, it has seven rooms, the
living-room is very big.**

Page 83

B **Restaurants:** 1-C, 2-A, 3-B

Practice: 1-BD, 2-AD, 3-CF, 4-CE

Q pollo = meat (chicken); merluza = fish (hake);
ternera = meat (veal); albóndigas = meat (meat-
balls); trucha = fish (trout); sardinas = fish
(sardines)

Page 84

A **Introductions:** 4 = 7 personas; 5 = 2 hermanos;
6 = 2 hermanas; 7 = un burro

B **Numbers and dates:** Carolina is 11 years old and
her birthday is 23 December.
Eduar is 12 years old and his birthday is 30 August.
Sarita is 15 years old.
Yimer is 13 years old.

Q 2 dos, 12 doce, 22 veintidós, 204 doscientos y
cuatro, 14 catorce, 40 cuarenta, 400 cuatro cientos

Page 85

C **Personal Information**

C3: 1+6, 2+7, 3+9, 5+10

Q quite tall - bastante alto/a; very slim - muy
delgado/a; your hair was very long - tengo el pelo
muy largo

Practice: 1-C, 2-E, 3-Y, 4-S, 5-Y

Page 86

A **Sports:** A 2 ticks; B 4 ticks; C 1 tick; D 3 ticks;
E 1 tick

Q bailar, patinar, leer, hacer gimnásia

B **Free time:** 1-V, 2-M, 3-V, 4-V, 5-M, 6-V, 7-M

Page 87

C **Arranging to go out:** True sentences are 1, 3, 5

Practice: 1-M, 2-ND, 3-V, 4-ND, 5-M

Q los fines de semana - the weekends, entresemana -
during the week, la semana que viene - next week

Page 88

A **Home town:** a-19, b-30, c-2000, d-1/4,
e-1/2

B **Likes and dislikes:** 1 pueblo - es más tranquilo.
2 ciudad - es más grande/hay más cosas que hacer.
3 pueblo - le gusta el campo y los animales.

Page 89

C **Your region:** In this order - 10, 7, 9, 2, 5, 1

Q They mention several bars.

Practice: Juanjo - positivo + es limpio/todo el
mundo le conoce.
Nerea - negativo + es demasiado pequeño.
Clara - negativa + le hacen falta (= no hay)
muchas cosas para los jóvenes.

Page 90

A **Directions:** la farmacia = b; la panadería = c;
la zapatería = a

Page 91

B **Shopping:** (Multiple choice) 1-a, 2-b, 3-a, 4-b,
5-c, 6-a

Q Vanesa asks if she can try it on. The shop assistant
thinks it's very pretty/nice.

Practice: 1 Laura thinks fashion is very important
2 autumn 3 going to school 4 go shopping
5 He likes it

C A-5, B-6, C-2, D-1, E-3, F-4

D (In this order) 4, 5, 3, 10, 2, 6

E Ticks for sentences 2, 4, 5

C 1-d, 2-a, 3-e, 4-c

D 1-P+N, 2-N, 3-P+N

E 1-E, 2-F, 3-A, 4-B, 5-C

C Quisiera un folleto sobre la ciudad, ¿Por dónde se va a la piscina? ¿A qué hora se cierra? Estoy aquí de vacaciones.

D Tengo sed, Quiero beber ... (any appropriate drink), Quisiera comer ... (two appropriate items of food), ¿Te gustaría ir al cine más tarde?

A/some: un hermano, una hermana, unos hombres, unas mujeres

The: el tío, la tía, los chicos, las chicas

Plural nouns: 30 libros, 15 mesas. 4 tablones, 3 ordenadores, 8 luces, 2 estantes, 5 pósters

Adjectives: italiana, catalana, escocesa, española, marrón, rosa

Gustar: Me gusta el dibujo. No me gusta la historia. Me gustan las matemáticas. No me gustan los deberes.

Indirect object pronouns: you like - te gusta/n, he/she/you likes - le gusta(n), we like - nos gusta(n), they like you - les gusta(n)

Present tense: (tú) hablas, (él, ella, usted) habla, (ellos, ellas, usted) hablan, (yo) como, (nosotros) comemos, (yo) vivo, (tú) vives, (vosotros) vivís

Irregular present tense: dar - doy, conocer - conozco, hacer - hago, poner - pongo, saber - sé, salir - salgo, traer - traigo, ver - veo

Use **estar** to indicate position, and temporary moods. Use **ser** for describing people, places, things.

Ir: vas, vamos, van

Tener: tengo, tiene, tenéis

Estar: estoy, estás, estamos, están

Ser: eres, es, sois, son

The immediate future: Use the verb **ir** followed by **a**, and the infinitive of another verb.

A/De

(a) When followed by **el** it becomes **al**.

(b) When followed by **el** it becomes **del**.

Reflexive verbs: (yo) me, (tú) te, (él, ella, usted) se, (ellos, ellas, ustedes) se

Question words: ¿dónde?, ¿cuánto?, ¿cómo?, ¿qué?, ¿cuándo?, ¿quién(es)?, ¿por qué?

Positive commands: (tú) come, escribe; (usted) hable, coma; escriba (tú) tuerce, sigue, (usted) cruce, coja, siga

The perfect tense: dejado, comido, salido, he hecho, he escrito, he puesto, he roto, he visto, (ha muerto)

The regular preterite tense: yo hablé, tú hablaste, él, ella, usted habló, ellos, ellas, ustedes hablarán; tú comiste, nosotros comimos, vosotros comisteis; yo viví, él, ella, usted vivió, ellos, ellas, ustedes vivieron

Irregular preterite verbs: ser/ir - fuiste, fuimos, fueron; **dar** - di, dio, disteis

The 'pretérito grave' stems: hic-, pud-, pus-, quis-, tuv-, vin-; tú -iste, nosotros -imos, yo -estuve, ellos, ellas, ustedes -ieron

Direct object pronouns: singulars - te, lo, la; **plurals** - nos, los, les

Direct object pronouns usually come before the verb.

They can be added on to the end of an infinitive.

Demonstrative adjectives: (this, *fs*) esta, (that, *ms*) ese, (that there, *fs*) aquella, (these, *mpl*) estos, (those, *fpl*) esas, (those there, *mpl*) aquellos

Demonstrative pronouns (this/that one, these/those ones) are the same as the adjectives above, but have an accent on the first 'e'.

Verbs of obligation: (have to, must) tener que, (ought to, should) deber, (one has to) hay que

Se ... : se + the third part of the verb ...; se come, se bebe, se escribe

The regular imperfect tense: (tú) hablabas, (nosotros) hablábamos, (ellos, ellas, ustedes) hablaban; (yo) bebía, (él, ella, usted) bebía, (vosotros) bebíais, (tú) vivías, (nosotros) vivíamos, (ellos, ellas, ustedes) vivían

Irregular imperfect tense verbs

Ir: íbas, iba, íbais, iban **Ser:** era, era, éramos, eran
Ver: veías, veía, veíamos, veían

The gerund and continuous tenses:
-ar verbs: -ando   (andando)
-er verbs: -iendo   (comiendo)
-ir verbs: -iendo   (escribiendo)

Present continuous: use the present tense of the verb **estar** + gerund

Imperfect continuous: use the imperfect tense of the verb **estar** + gerund

The future and conditional tenses: The future tense indicates what will happen. The conditional indicates what would happen. The endings are the same for -ar, -er, -ir verbs.

Future: (tú) hablarás, (nosotros) hablaremos, (ellos, ellas, ustedes) hablarán

Conditional: (yo) hablaría, (él, ella, usted) hablaría, (vosotros) hablaríais

Irregular future/conditional stems: har-, podr-, pondr-, querr-, tendr-, vendr-

Relative pronouns: que (who, that, which), quien(es) (who), lo que (what, that which)

Ser/estar: ser - 2 jobs/professions; **estar** - 1 temporary states; 3 position/place

Negative commands: (tú) - no comas, no escribas, (usted) no hable, no coma, no escriba

Impersonal verbs: to hurt - doler; to delight - encantar; to be lacking - faltar; to be necessary - hacer falta; to interest - interesar; to remain; be left over - quedar; to be an excess of - sobrar

Me duele la espalda; Te encanta el deporte, ¿no?; Le falta un cuchillo; Nos hace falta más dinero; Os interesa mucho el tenis, creo; Quedan tres manzanas.

Sobra vino.

Adverbs: To form adverbs, take the masculine form of the adjective. Now make it feminine and add -mente: rápido, rápida, rápidamente; lento, lenta, lentamente; fácil, fácil, fácilmente

Well - bien; badly - mal; slowly - despacio

There are two words for quickly: rápido, rápidamente

Check your grammar in the exam

Gender of nouns: do I need el, la, los or las? Should it be un, una, unos, unas?

The word for 'to/at' is **a**; followed by **el**, it becomes **al**

The word for 'of/from' is **de**: followed by **el**, it becomes **del**.

Endings on adjectives: masculine, feminine, singular, plural

Endings on verbs: is this the correct tense?

Impersonal verbs like **gustar** need an indirect object pronoun: should it be **me, te, le, nos, os, les**?

Direct object pronouns: use **le** and **les** for people, and **lo, la, los, las** for things.

Last-minute learner

- The next four pages give you the key vocabulary across the whole subject in the smallest possible space.
- You can use these pages as a final check.
- You can also use them as you revise as a way to check your learning.
- You can cut them out for quick and easy reference.

Numbers

1	uno	14	catorce	27	veintisiete	101	ciento uno
2	dos	15	quince	28	veintiocho	200	doscientos
3	tres	16	dieciséis	29	veintinueve	300	trescientos
4	cuatro	17	diecisiete	30	treinta	400	cuatrocientos
5	cinco	18	dieciocho	31	treinta y uno	500	quinientos
6	seis	19	diecinueve	32	treinta y dos	600	seiscientos
7	siete	20	veinte	40	cuarenta	700	setecientos
8	ocho	21	veintiuno	50	cincuenta	800	ochocientos
9	nueve	22	veintidós	60	sesenta	900	novecientos
10	diez	23	veintitrés	70	setenta	1000	mil
11	once	24	veinticuatro	80	ochenta		
12	doce	25	veinticinco	90	noventa		
13	trece	26	veintiséis	100	cien		

Days of the week

lunes	*Monday*
martes	*Tuesday*
miércoles	*Wednesday*
jueves	*Thursday*
viernes	*Friday*
sábado	*Saturday*
domingo	*Sunday*
el fin de semana	*weekend*

Months of the year

enero	*January*	julio	*July*
febrero	*February*	agosto	*August*
marzo	*March*	septiembre	*September*
abril	*April*	octubre	*October*
mayo	*May*	noviembre	*November*
junio	*June*	diciembre	*December*

Me and my family (pp. 8, 9, 12)

- Me presento. Me llamo (John Brown). Mi nombre/apellido se escribe (J-O-H-N). Tengo (quince) años. Mi cumpleaños es el (quince) de (mayo). De nacionalidad, soy (escocés). Soy (alto), y (delgado). Tengo los ojos (azules) y el pelo (corto, marrón y liso). Tengo pecas. Llevo (gafas, lentes de contacto).
- ¿Cúantas personas hay en tu familia? En mi familia, somos (seis) personas. Mis padres están (divorciados) y vivo con mi (madre), mi (padrastro), mis dos hermanos que se llaman (David) y (Chris) y mi hermana, que se llama (Alison).
- ¡Hola! ¿Qué tal? Fenomenal, estupendo, regular/voy tirando, no muy bien, fatal. Te/le presento a mi (madre, mejor amigo). Encantado/a de conocerte/le. ¡Pasa/pase! ¡Bienvenido/a!). Muchas gracias por su hospitalidad.

Interests and hobbies (pp. 9, 14, 15)

- ¿Qué deportes practicas? En mi tiempo libre, juego (al fútbol) y (al baloncesto). ¿Qué te gusta hacer (en invierno/verano?) En verano, practico (el atletismo) y (el piragüismo). En (invierno), me gusta (hacer judo), y (escuchar música).

- ¿Qué te gusta hacer en tu tiempo libre? Me encanta (navegar por Internet) porque es (interesante) pero no me gusta mucho (ver la tele) — es (aburrido). ¿Tocas algún instrumento? No toco ningún instrumento, pero me gustaría aprender a tocar (la batería). Toco (la guitarra) un poco. ¿Te gustaría (jugar, salir) con nosotros? Sí, con mucho gusto.

Home (pp. 9, 16, 17)

- ¿Dónde vives? Vivo en (Sherington), (una ciudad) en el (noroeste) de (Inglaterra). Mi (casa) está (en una urbanización) en las afueras. Vivo en (una casa adosada) de (dos) plantas. Abajo hay (la cocina, el salón, el comedor, y el lavadero), y arriba hay (el cuarto de baño y tres dormitorios). Delante hay (un jardín pequeño y un garaje), y detrás está (el patio) y (un jardín más grande).

Your bedroom (pp. 9, 17)

- ¿Tienes tu propio dormitorio? Sí, tengo mi propio dormitorio. No, tengo que compartir con (mi hermana). Mi dormitorio es (bastante pequeño), y (pintado/empapelado) en (azul y verde). Hay una ventana que da (al jardín). Detrás de la puerta está (la cama), y (una mesilla de noche) con (una lámpara). Debajo de la ventana, hay (un escritorio) donde (hago mis deberes). Hay también un guardarropa y un tocador para mis cosas, y un estante para mis libros y CDs.

Daily routine (pp. 18, 20, 21, 22, 23)

- ¿A qué hora te levantas? Me levanto (a las siete) (entresemana, el fin de semana). ¿Qué llevas para ir al instituto? Llevo (un uniforme: un pantalón gris ...) ¿Cómo vas al instituto? Voy (en autobús), mi (padre) me lleva en coche. ¿A qué hora sales de casa? Salgo (a las ocho). ¿Cuánto tiempo tardas en llegar? Tardo (veinte) minutos.
- ¿A qué hora empiezan las clases? Empiezan (a las nueve). ¿Cuántas clases hay por día? Hay (seis). ¿Cuánto tiempo dura cada clase? Las clases duran (una hora). ¿Cuándo hay recreos? Hay recreos (a las once) y (a la una). ¿A qué hora terminan las clases? Terminan (a las cuatro). ¿Dónde comes al mediodía? Como (en la cantina). Vuelvo a casa para comer.
- ¿Cuándo vuelves a casa por la tarde? Vuelvo a (las cuatro y media).
- ¿Cuántas horas de deberes haces? Hago (tres) horas de deberes. ¿Qué te gusta hacer por la tarde? Me gusta (ver la tele.) ¿A qué hora te acuestas? Me acuesto a (las once).
- ¿Qué diferencias hay en tu rutina de lunes a viernes y el fin de semana? El (sábado) (me levanto tarde), y por la noche (salgo con mis amigos). Vamos a la (bolera, pista de hielo).

Meals and mealtimes (pp. 20, 21, 23)

- ¿A qué hora (desayunas, comes, cenas)? (Desayuno, como, ceno) a (las ocho). ¿Dónde sueles cenar? Suelo (cenar, comer) en (el comedor, la cocina, delante de la tele). ¿Qué tipo de comida te gusta? Me gusta (la carne) y me encantan (las pastas). Soy vegetariano/a. Soy alérgico/a a (la leche). (Odio, detesto, no aguanto) (las verduras).

School subjects, buildings, next year (pp. 19, 24, 25)

- En total, estudio (ocho) asignaturas: (cinco) obligatorios y (tres) optativos. Estudio (la lengua y literatura ...). Me gusta mucho (el dibujo) porque es (fácil), (la profesora) es (divertida) y (saco buenas notas). Odio (la física) porque soy muy flojo/a en esta asignatura.
- Mi instituto es (bastante grande) y (moderno). Tiene muchas aulas, laboratorios, (dos) cocinas, (tres) sala(s) de ordenadores, una biblioteca, un patio, un gimnasio y un campo de deporte. Después de los exámenes, voy a (seguir mis estudios) aquí y (hacer los A levels). En verano, quiero (descansar un rato). Me gustaría (ganar dinero) y (pasarlo bien).

Asking the way (pp. 26, 32–33)

- ¿Hay (un bar/una farmacia) por aquí? Sí, hay (uno/una) en (la Plaza Mayor).
- ¿Por dónde se va al (castillo)? Tome/coja (la primera) a la (izquierda), tuerza (a la derecha), cruce (el puente), siga todo recto hasta (los semáforos, el final de la calle) y está allí, (enfrente de la comisaría).

Travel and transport (pp. 26, 27, 30, 31, 57)

- Quisiera/quiero comprar un billete (sencillo, de ida y vuelta) para (Burgos), de (segunda) clase, y (no fumador). ¿Cuánto cuesta (un bonobús?). ¿A qué hora llega (el tren de Marbella)? ¿A qué hora sale (el autocar para Madrid)? ¿De qué andén sale? ¿Hay que cambiar/hacer transbordo? ¿Cuánto tiempo tarda en llegar? ¿Hay que pagar un suplemento? ¿Dónde puedo (dejar la maleta, comprar una revista)? (La consigna, el quiosco) está (allí).

Weather (pp. 27, 34, 35)

- ¿Qué tiempo hace? Hace buen/mal tiempo. ¿Qué dice el pronóstico? Hace/hará (frío, calor, mucho sol, viento). Hay/habrá (lluvia, neblina, niebla, granizo, tormenta). Llueve, nieva. El cielo está (despejado, nublado).

Home town. Tourism (pp. 20, 21, 27, 34, 35)

• Mi (barrio) es (antiguo) pero (ruidoso). Para divertirse hay (el cine). Para comprar (hay el centro comerical). La gente es (simpática) pero/y (no) hay mucho para (los jóvenes). De día, se puede (acampar, visitar ..., explorar ...). De noche, se puede (ir a la discoteca). Mi ciudad ideal tendría (más lugares verdes, buenas instalaciones, más distracciones). Lo bueno es que (es bonito). Lo malo es que (no hay nada para los jóvenes). El problema es que hay mucho/a (desempleo, basura, ruido).

Holidays (pp. 36, 40–41)

• Fui a (España) en (avión) con (mi familia). Pasé/pasamos (quince días) en (un hotel) cerca de (la playa). (El hotel) era (cómodo) y la comida era (buena).

• De día, fui (a la playa) donde tomé el sol y nadé (en el mar). Un día, hice/hicimos una excursión (en autocar) a (la sierra). Me gustó mucho (el ambiente) y (el tiempo): lo pasé bomba/me divertí mucho. Algo que no me gustó fue (la basura en las calles).

Accommodation (pp. 36, 38, 39)

• ¿Dónde está la Oficina de Turismo? ¿Tiene (un folleto sobre la ciudad, una lista de hoteles, un horario de autobuses)? ¿A qué hora se abre/cierra (el museo)? Estoy/estamos aquí de vacaciones. ¿Qué hay que ver en (la ciudad/región)?

• ¿Tiene habitaciones libres? Quisiera reservar (una habitación individual) para esta noche/(dos noches) desde el (cinco) de (julio) hasta el (siete). ¿El desayuno/el almuerzo está incluido? ¿A qué hora se sirve (la cena)? Quisiera una habitación con (balcón, vista del mar). ¿Hay sitio para (una tienda familiar)? ¿Dónde se puede (aparcar, dejar la basura, cocinar)? Firme la ficha por favor.

Restaurants (pp. 36, 41)

• ¿Me/Nos trae el menú/la carta/la lista de vinos, por favor? ¿Qué quiere tomar (de primero, de segundo, de postre, para beber)? Quisiera, para mi, para mi (amigo/a) ... ¿Qué hay para vegetarianos? ¿Qué es ... exactamente? ¿Contiene ...? El (plato)/la (cuchara) está sucio/a. Falta un (tenedor)/una (taza).

• ¿Me/nos trae más agua/pan por favor? ¿El servicio está incluido? ¿Se puede pagar con tarjeta de crédito?

Feeling ill (pp. 36, 42)

• No me siento/encuentro bien. ¿Qué te/le pasa? Tengo (un catarro, tos, náuseas, fiebre). Me duele el (brazo)/la garganta. Me duelen los (pies)/las (muelas). ¿Desde hace cuánto tiempo no te sientes/se siente bien? Desde ayer, desde hace (dos) días. Tome (este jarabe, esta medicina, estas pastillas, estos antibióticos), ponga (esta crema, estas tiritas). Hay que tomar (dos) cucharaditas (tres) veces al día. ¿Puede venir a verme mañana?

Lost property (p. 43)

• He perdido/Acabo de perder mi (bolsa, máquina fotográfica, mochila). Me han robado (el monedero). ¿Dónde lo/la perdió? Creo que lo/la perdí (en el cine). ¿Cómo lo/la perdió? Estaba (viendo la película, mirando la tele, hablando con mis amigos). Mi (bolsa) estaba en (el suelo, mi silla, a mi lado). No sé cómo/qué ocurrió exactamente.

• ¿Cómo era? Era (azul), de (cuero) y bastante (pequeño). ¿Qué contenía? Contenía (mis llaves, mi pasaporte, mi monedero, mi billete de avión). ¿Puede usted volver mañana? Lo siento, voy a volver a (Gran Bretaña).

Household chores (pp. 44, 49)

• ¿Tienes que ayudar en casa? ¿Qué tienes que hacer? Tengo que (hacer mi cama) (todos los días, el fin de semana). ¿Qué tiene que hacer tu (hermano)? — Tiene que (lavar/fregar los platos). ¿Hay algún quehacer que no te guste?

• Odio/detesto (poner la mesa) porque es (aburrido, pesado).

Healthy living (pp. 44, 48)

• ¿Qué haces/que hay que hacer para (estar sano/a, en forma)? ¿Qué vas a hacer tú? Hago/voy a hacer (más) ejercicio, como/voy a seguir un régimen sano. Hay que (beber menos alcohol). Se debe (dormir siete horas al día). Hace falta (respetar el cuerpo). Sería mejor/es importante no (fumar, emborracharse). Es (peligroso/dañino) (tomar drogas). Es (bueno) para la salud (evitar demasiado estrés, tomar comida nutritiva).

Leisure (pp. 45, 50–51)

• ¿Qué ponen el la tele/el cine? Ponen (una película de ciencia-ficción).

• ¿Qué tipo de programa te gusta más? Me gustan (los dibujos animados). No me gustan mucho (los documentales). ¿Ves mucho la tele? Veo (dos) horas al día, más/menos el fin de semana. Soy muy aficionado/a a las telenovelas.

• ¿Cuánto cuestan las entradas? ¿A qué hora empieza/termina (la sesión)? ¿Te gustaría ir (al cine)? Sí, buena idea. No puedo. Tengo que (hacer los deberes, cuidar a mi hermano/a). No me interesa mucho. No tengo (ganas, tiempo, dinero). ¿A qué hora nos vemos? ¿Si nos vemos a (las ocho)?

Contacting others (pp. 55, 56–57)

- ¡Diga! ¡Dígame! ¡Oiga! ¿Está (Raúl)? ¿Me pone con (Ana)? ¿De parte de quién? De parte (del Señor Alonso). Está comunicando. No contesta. ¿Cuál es el número/prefijo? ¿Qué número hay que marcar? Es el (92. 22. 51. 67).
- ¿Puedo dejar un recado?

Shopping (pp. 45, 52–53)

- ¿Dónde puedo comprar (un cinturón)? Busco (una camiseta) ¿Tiene (gafas de sol)? ¿Se venden (cajas de turrón)? ¿Hay pan (fresco)? Lo siento, no queda(n). Quisiera (cien gramos) de (queso), (una lata) de (tomates). ¿Me pone/da (un kilo de manzanas) por favor?
- ¿Qué tamaño? Grande, pequeño, mediano. ¿Qué talla usa? La (40). ¿Qué número calza? El (38). No me queda(n) bien, no me va(n) bien. Es demasiado (estrecho/a, ancho/a, largo/a, corto/a). No me gusta el color.
- Me lo/la/los/las llevo.
- ¿Es todo? Sí, es todo. ¿Algo más? No, nada más, gracias. ¿Tiene cambio? No, lo siento, no tengo cambio. Sólo tengo un billete de (50) euros. ¿Se puede pagar con (un cheque, con tarjeta de crédito, en metálico/efectivo).

Part-time jobs (pp. 54, 58–59)

- ¿Tienes algún empleo? ¿Cuándo trabajas? Trabajo todos los días, el fin de semana desde (las ocho) hasta (la una). ¿Cuántas horas trabajas? Trabajo (seis horas) al día. ¿Cuándo empiezas/terminas? Empiezo/termino a (la una)
- ¿Cuánto ganas? Gano (tres libras esterlinas) por hora/al día. ¿Qué opinas del trabajo? Es (interesante) pero (mal pagado).

Work experience (pp. 54, 60–61)

- ¿Dónde hiciste tu experiencia laboral? La hice/trabajé en (una oficina).
- ¿Cuánto tiempo duró? Duró (diez) días.
- ¿Cómo ibas a tu lugar de trabajo? Iba (andando).
- ¿Cuánto tiempo tardabas en llegar? Tardaba unos (20) minutos.
- ¿Cómo era el horario? Empezaba/ terminaba a las (nueve).
- ¿Qué tenías que hacer? Tenía que (archivar, coger el teléfono).
- ¿Te gustó? Lo bueno era que (la gente era simpática), lo malo era que (el trabajo era repetitivo). Me divertí/me aburrí mucho.

Character and relationships (pp. 62, 66, 67)

- De carácter, ¿cómo eres? Soy (amable) y (un poco perezoso). ¿Cómo es tu (padre/madre)? Mi (padre/madre) es (simpático/a). ¿Cuáles son las características de (un/a buen/a amigo/a)? Él/ella debe ser (honrado/a).

- ¿Qué tal las relaciones en tu familia? Son buenas/malas. ¿Te llevas bien con (tu hermano)? (No) me llevo bien con (mi hermana) porque (me irrita, me fastidia, me hace subir por las paredes). Me enfado con él, ella, mi (hermana).
- Su (comportamiento, conducta) es (bueno/a, malo/a).

Environment (pp. 63, 68, 69)

- ¿Qué debemos hacer para proteger el medio ambiente? (No) debemos/deberíamos (utilizar) (tanto vidrio). Debe haber más (contenadores para reciclar). Me preocupo/inquieto por (la contaminación/la polución). Sería mejor (reciclar) (más cosas). Vamos a (destrozar) (la naturaleza).

Education issues (pp. 63, 70, 71)

- ¿Adónde quieres ir para seguir tus/sus estudios ? Quiero/Espero ir a (la universidad). Me gustaría hacer una carrera en (el derecho).
- ¿Qué opinas de tener reglas/normas? Creo que las reglas son (necesarias).
- ¿Hay algo que cambiarías? No estoy a favor (del uniforme).
- ¿Qué opinas de la disciplina en tu instituto? Creo que (es buena).
- ¿Cuáles son las ventajas de ir al instituto? La ventaja más grande es que (sales con buenas calificaciones).

Work, career and future plans (pp. 72, 74–77)

- ¿Qué planes tienes para el futuro? ¿En qué te gustaría trabajar? Quiero (ser comerciante). Me gustaría trabajar en el sector de (la industria). Preferiría (viajar en el extranjero). Tendré que (pedir un préstamo). Me interesa un trabajo (científico, físico, artístico).
- ¿En que trabajan tus padres? Mi madre/padre es (mecánico/a).

Social issues, choices and responsibilities (pp. 72, 78–79)

- Los problemas sociales más importantes de hoy en día son (el paro y la guerra). Lo que más me preocupa es (la droga/el SIDA). Muy importante es (la presión del grupo paritario). Tenemos que hacer más/algo diferente para ayudar a los que (toman drogas).